HISTORY OF KA'ABA
(A Unique Research on the History of Ka'aba)

The Name of Book : History of Ka'aba

Author : Muhammad Salih bin Ahmad bin Zainul Abideen Sheebi
Al Abadri Al Hajabi

Research and Compilation : Rauf Siddiqui.

Translation : S. M. Mahboob-ul-Hassan Bukhari & Rauf Siddiqui

Composing : Hafiz Muhammad Imran Qureshi.

Publisher : 3 Star Publisher., Karachi-Pakistan. Tel: 021-32768227

Third Issuance : 20 Jamadi-ul-Awwal (1431 H), 05 May, 2010

Quantity : 1000

Price in Pak Rs: 450/=

Price in Foreign Currencies:

Doha, Qatar   : 19.5 Riyals   U.A.E. : 19.5 Dirhams

Muscat, Oman: 02 Riyals   U.K.   : 3.5 Pounds Sterling

Saudi Arabia : 20 Riyals   U.S.A., Canada : 5.5 Dollars

ISBN No. : 978-969-8894-05-4

Postal Address:
B-123/10 Federal B. Area, Karachi-38, Pakistan.
0092-21-6366895
www.raufsiddiqui.pk
raufsiddiqui@raufsiddiqui.pk

S.B 21717. Riyadh 11485, Saudi Arabia.

HISTORY
OF
KA'ABA

(A Unique Research on the History of Ka'aba)

In the name of Allah, the most Gracious, the most Merciful.

Dedication

This book is dedicated to all mankind
from Adam (blessings of Allah be
upon him) upto the last day.

Rauf Siddiqui.

History
of Ka'aba

Contents

Acknowledgements	09
Preamble by (Rauf Siddiqui)	10
Dignity of Ka'aba in the light of Holy Qur'an	10
Dignity of Ka'aba in the light of Ahadith	14
Preface	23
The Respect for Ka'aba before and after Islam	24
Measurements of Ka'aba	26
Famous constructioins of Ka'aba	28
Construction by Adam	29
Construction by Ibrahim and Ismaeel	38
Construction by Quraish	50
Construction by Abdullah bin Zubair	58
Completion of construction of Ka'aba	63
Construction by Hujjaj bin Yousaf	65
Construction by Sultan Murad Khan the IV	67
History of Renovations and Inscrtiptions in Ka'aba	70
Covering of Ka'aba	77
Covering of Ka'aba by Abasaid Caliphs and Kings	81
Covering of Ka'aba by Kings of Egypt and Yaman	82
Covering of Ka'aba by the Emperors of Ottoman Empire	83
Writing on the cover of Ka'aba	85
The Ruling for the use of the covers of Ka'aba	89
Gifts and Hanged Objects in Ka'aba	91
Theft of the objects of Ka'aba	93
Entering Ka'aba and offering prayer	94
The Ruling for prayer in Ka'aba	98
Key Bearers of Ka'aba in the time of ignorance	101
Qusai bin Kalab as custodian of Makkah	103
Key Bearers of Ka'aba in Islam	105
Interpretation of the Verse 58 of Al Nisa	106
The saying of Holy Prophet about Key Bearing	111
The verdicts of Scholars about Services, Covers & Gifts	112
The decision of Scholars and Authorities about Ka'aba	119
Sheeba bin Uthman	120
The Decision of Authorities and Scholars	123
The Key Bearers of Ka'aba	126
The Lineage of Holy Prophet Muhammad	128
Viewing of Ka'aba is a worship	128

Acknowledgement of Gratitude

Letters of thanks received from many

Heads of States in acknowledgment

of receipt of the book

"THE HISTORY OF KA'ABA"

Letter from Prime Minister of The Hashemite
Kingdom of Jordan — 164

Letter from President of the Council of Ministers
Lebanese Republic — 165

Letter from Prime Minister of People's Democratic
Republic of Algeria — 166

Translation of Letter from Prime Minister of
People's Democratic Republic of Algeria — 167

Letter from The Head of the Cabinet of the
President of the French Republic — 168

Translation of Letter from The Head of the
Cabinet of the President of the French Republic — 169

Letter from the President The Republic of Tunisia — 170

Translation of Letter from The President
The Republic of Tunisia — 171

Letter from the President of United States of America — 172

Acknowledgements

I am grateful to many people who have helped me in translating this book. I gratefully thank Mr. Rauf Siddiqui who placed trust in me and encouraged me like a friendly brother. Professor Zahid Siddique read and made helpful comments on a large chunk of my draft of translation. Special thanks are also due to my fellow professor Kamran Qureshi for his patience and encouragement throughout. I owe a continuing debt to my teachers and students. Finally I am greatly indebted to my family for their good–humoured endurance for my preoccupation with this work.

S. M. Mahboob-ul-Hassan Bukhari

Lecturer at Institute of Business Management, Karachi.

Preamble
by Rauf Siddiqui

Dignity of Ka'aba
in the light of Holy Qur'an

I begin with relevant verses of Holy Qur'an and traditions of Holy Prophet Muhammad (peace and blessings of Allah be upon him) that will shed a flood of light on the dignity of Holy Ka'aba.

وَإِذْ جَعَلْنَا الْبَيْتَ مَثَابَةً لِّلنَّاسِ وَأَمْنًا ۖ وَاتَّخِذُوا مِنْ مَّقَامِ اِبْرٰهٖمَ مُصَلًّى ۖ وَعَهِدْنَآ اِلٰٓى اِبْرٰهٖمَ وَاِسْمٰعِيْلَ اَنْ طَهِّرَا بَيْتِيَ لِلطَّآئِفِيْنَ وَالْعٰكِفِيْنَ وَالرُّكَّعِ السُّجُوْدِ ۞ وَاِذْ قَالَ اِبْرٰهٖمُ رَبِّ اجْعَلْ هٰذَا بَلَدًا اٰمِنًا وَّارْزُقْ اَهْلَهٗ مِنَ الثَّمَرٰتِ مَنْ اٰمَنَ مِنْهُمْ بِاللّٰهِ وَالْيَوْمِ الْاٰخِرِ ۖ قَالَ وَمَنْ كَفَرَ فَاُمَتِّعُهٗ قَلِيْلًا ثُمَّ اَضْطَرُّهٗۤ اِلٰى عَذَابِ النَّارِ ۖ وَبِئْسَ الْمَصِيْرُ ۞ وَاِذْ يَرْفَعُ اِبْرٰهٖمُ الْقَوَاعِدَ مِنَ الْبَيْتِ وَاِسْمٰعِيْلُ ۖ رَبَّنَا تَقَبَّلْ مِنَّا ۖ اِنَّكَ اَنْتَ السَّمِيْعُ الْعَلِيْمُ ۞ رَبَّنَا وَاجْعَلْنَا مُسْلِمَيْنِ لَكَ وَمِنْ ذُرِّيَّتِنَآ اُمَّةً مُّسْلِمَةً لَّكَ ۖ وَاَرِنَا مَنَاسِكَنَا وَتُبْ عَلَيْنَا ۖ اِنَّكَ اَنْتَ التَّوَّابُ الرَّحِيْمُ ۞

And when we made the House (at Makkah) a resort for mankind and a sanctuary (saying): Take as your place of worship the place where Abraham stood (to pray). And we imposed a duty upon Abraham and

Ishmael, (saying): Purify My House for those who go around and those who mediate therein and those who bow and prostrate themselves (in worship).

"And when Abraham prayed: My Lord! Make this a region of security and bestow upon its people fruits, such of them as believe in Allah and the Last Day, He answered: As for him who disbelieveth, I shall leave him in contentment for a while, then I shall compel him to the doom of fire--a hapless journey's end!"

"And when Abraham and Ishmael were raising the foundations of the House, (Abraham prayed): Our Lord! Accept from us (this duty). Lo! Thou, only Thou, art the Hearer, the Knower."

"Our Lord! And make us submissive unto Thee and of our seed a nation submissive unto Thee, and show us our ways of worship, and relent toward us. Lo! Thou, only Thou, art the Relenting, the Merciful."[1]

Allah declares Ka'aba to be the Qibla of Muslims. Allah says in Holy Qur'an.

﴿ قَدْ نَرَى تَقَلُّبَ وَجْهِكَ فِى السَّمَآءِ ۖ فَلَنُوَلِّيَنَّكَ قِبْلَةً تَرْضَىٰهَا ۚ فَوَلِّ وَجْهَكَ شَطْرَ الْمَسْجِدِ الْحَرَامِ ۚ وَحَيْثُ مَا كُنْتُمْ فَوَلُّوا وُجُوهَكُمْ شَطْرَهُ ط ﴾

"We have seen the turning of thy face to heaven (for guidance, O Muhammad). And now

---

[1] Al Baqara:125,126,127,128

verily We shall make thee turn (in prayer) toward a qiblah which is dear to thee. So turn thy face toward the Inviolable Place of Worship, and ye (O Muslims), wheresoever ye may be, turn your faces (when ye pray) toward it.[1]

Muslim worshiped with face towards Bait-ul-Maqdis for few months. Jews and Christians, too, worshiped in that direction. This verse has altered the direction of Qibla from Bait-ul-Maqdis to Ka'aba for Muslims. Allah has described the honor of this house in the following verse.

﴿ وَلَا تُقَاتِلُوهُمْ عِنْدَ الْمَسْجِدِ الْحَرَامِ حَتَّىٰ يُقَاتِلُوكُمْ فِيهِ ﴾

"And fight not with them at the Inviolable Place of Worship until they first attack you there."[2]

Allah says at another place

---

[1] Al Baqara:144
[2] Al Baqara: 191

﴿ يَسْـَٔلُونَكَ عَنِ الشَّهْرِ الْحَرَامِ قِتَالٍ فِيهِ ۖ قُلْ قِتَالٌ فِيهِ كَبِيرٌ ۖ وَصَدٌّ عَنْ سَبِيلِ اللّٰهِ وَكُفْرٌ بِهِ وَالْمَسْجِدِ الْحَرَامِ وَإِخْرَاجُ أَهْلِهِ مِنْهُ أَكْبَرُ عِنْدَ اللّٰهِ ۚ ﴾

"They question thee (O Muhammad) with regard to warfare in the sacred month. Say: Warfare therein is a great (transgression), but to turn (men) from the way of Allah, and to disbelieve in Him and in the Inviolable Place of Worship, and to expel his people thence, is a greater with Allah." [1]

This verse was revealed about non believers who used to stop Muslims from circumambulation of the sacred house. They would drag them out of the mosque Al Haram. Muslims in general and Muhammad (peace and blessings of Allah be upon him) in particular was advised to preach the message of Allah in such a way that people may happily enter the fold of Islam. Hence Allah almighty says

﴿ وَلَا يَجْرِمَنَّكُمْ شَنَآنُ قَوْمٍ أَنْ صَدُّوكُمْ عَنِ الْمَسْجِدِ الْحَرَامِ أَنْ تَعْتَدُوا ۘ ﴾

"And let not your hatred of a folk who (once) stopped your going to the Inviolable Place of Worship seduce you to transgress." [2]

---

[1] Al Baqara: 217
[2] Al Maeeda 2: 5

Dignity of Ka'aba
in the light of Ahadith

The following four traditions of Holy Prophet Muhammad (peace and blessings of Allah be upon him) indicate clearly the dignity of the House of Allah.

1. Abu Dhar says that I have inquired Prophet which was the first mosque ever made on the earth? He replied " mosque Al Haram"

2. Prophet Muhammad (peace and blessings of Allah be upon him) said my worship in this mosque is thousand times better than in others except in mosque Al Haram"

3. Prophet Muhammad (peace and blessings of Allah be upon him) said " Don't intend to travel to any mosques except three mosque: mosque AlHaram, mosque AlAqsa,and my mosque (mosque of Prophet) .

4. Abdul Abbas narrates that when Prophet entered the mosque AlHaram he offered prayers in every corner of it."

The above mentioned Qur'anic verses and the traditions of Holy Prophet Muhammad (peace and blessings of Allah be upon him) and many others indicate the fact that the House of Allah is not only honorable itself but also respectable for its constructors. The first constructor of the house of Allah is His beloved Prophet Adam (blessings of Allah be upon him). He was followed by Prophet Sheesh, Prophet Ibrahim (blessings of Allah be upon them) and Ismaeel (blessings of Allah be upon him). This House has been repaired many times in the history by many respected and honorable men. Even our Holy Prophet Muhammad (peace and blessings of Allah be upon him) was honored to participate in its rebuilding. After his demise the righteous Caliphs, Ummayads, Abbasides, Kings of Ottoman empire and the royal family of Saood have been serving this house with their invaluable services. King Abdul Aziz bin Abdur Rahman extended the area of Holy Ka'aba in 1956 A.D. (1375 Hijrah). King Fahad bin Abdul Aziz also extended the area of the mosque Al Haram in 1988 A.D. (1409 Hijrah). King Abdullah bin Abdul Aziz is also extending the area between Safa and Marwa. (The author was alive at the time and was writing this book) All revealed books and scriptures show that this is the first ever constructed building on the surface of earth. This implies that this is the House from where civilizations sprang. Allah almighty ordains Prophet Muhammad (peace and blessings of Allah be upon him) in these words.

﴿ قُلْ يَا أَهْلَ الْكِتٰبِ تَعَالَوْا إِلٰى كَلِمَةٍ سَوَآءٍ بَيْنَنَا وَبَيْنَكُمْ ﴾

Say: O People of the Scripture. Come to an agreement between us
and you: that we shall worship none but Allah[1].

This verse carries not only inter religious and inter cultural meanings
but also participates in all sociopolitical, ethicoreligious and geopolitical
treaties transcending religious sects. By that universal peace and
tranquility can be maintained. The word Kalima means that the public
in general be invited to the unity of Allah. Mankind has split up into
different religions today. It can only be integrated and united by the
belief in the unity of Allah. Our Holy Prophet Muhammad (peace and
blessings of Allah be upon him) invited everybody irrespective of his
cast, race, language, and historicity. This was for the first time
materialized by the father of all Prophets Adam (blessings of Allah be
upon him) on the earth in the shape of Ka'aba. It is the beginning of
a new chapter in the history of world.

_____

[1] Al-i-Imran: 64

Culture refers to the ways of life in a society. Islam does not propagate a certain culture or prefers one to other in any sense. Culture is inevitably linked with the social life and society of a certain individual. Islam is a universal religion. It can only flourish in the lands where ethics become the order of the day. The best example in this regard, is the amalgamation of Arabs and non-Arabs on the same platform of Islam. Civilizations sprang from the first man on earth. He was none other than the Prophet of Allah, Adam (Allah be pleased with him). He was the man who had actually taught people the principles of a successful life.

People are unconsciously nurtured by the dictates of history. Its norms, values, rites and rituals shape the personalities of the inhabitants. Values are of paramount importance in every civilized society. People even sacrifice their lives to sustain values. For peace and tranquility, these are inevitable in every society. Peace is vital to bring welfare in the life of mankind. This reminds us the event that took place in the life of our Holy Prophet Muhammad (peace and blessings of Allah be upon him) during the construction of Ka'aba. The tribes of Quraish reached the point when the black stone had to be replaced where it ought to be. A dispute arose as to who should get this honor. Everybody wanted to have it.

Even swords were unsheathed to prevent rivals doing that by force. An old sage intervened to calm the spirits. He said, "How can one shed blood in the sacred territory?" He proposed a solution: "Leave it to the providence, whoever turns up first let him arbitrate!" It was Muhammad (peace and blessings of Allah be upon him) and everybody hailed him and said: "The honest is coming, The honest is coming".

When he learnt the story of the dispute he asked for a sheet of cloth to be brought to him. He placed the sacred black stone on it and asked a representative of each and every tribe to raise the sheet of cloth. When it was brought near to the level where it had to be placed, he affixed the stone there with his own hands. Everybody was satisfied. The point is to be considered here. Muhammad (peace and blessings of Allah be upon him) could have fixed the Black Stone himself and none would have objected. But with the participation of every leader of Quraish, this dispute was resolved once for all. Hence before announcing that he was Prophet of Allah he brought peace to the Arabs in action and saved them from a possible war. It is a message to the world community from our Holy Prophet that every complex issue could be resolved if we act sincerely and wisely.

On the conquest of Makkah, our Holy Prophet Muhammad (peace and blessings of Allah be upon him) discharged the traces of the tasks of the days of ignorance, except the custodianship of the Ka'aba and the function of providing drinking water to pilgrims. Banu Abbas were responsible to provide drinking water to pilgrims. The family of Sheeba was the custodian of the Ka'aba. This responsibility is fulfilled with utmost sincerity and devotion by them generations after generations. I am fortunate enough to have a very good relation with the family of sheeba over the years. This might be the very reason that AbdurRehman Salih Zain-ul-Abideen AlShaibi gifted me this classical history of the Holy Ka'aba. This was written by Muhammad Salih Ahmad Bin Zaidn Al Al-Abideen in 1882 A.D.(1299 Hijrah). The moment I received this book, I intended to get it published not only in its original language Arabic but also in English and Urdu. Having been in three different common languages it could enlighten the hearts and souls of Muslims by the blessings of Allah across the globe. It could be fruitful to all Muslims in general and scholars in particular all over the world.

A lot of literature is available on this topic in many languages including English but this book is featured with its classical touch and at the same time being in the lucid language and approach.

In addition, it describes the history of the Key Bearers of the house of Allah comprehensively which is published for the first time in English. I have worked hard day in and day out to translate this work besides my busy schedule. This book is entitled "History of Ka'aba". I have also tried to make it more understandable to a layman as well as beneficial to intellectuals. Arabs have got a typical style of writing. They always mention the dates in lunar calendars which are not familiar to us. In order to overcome this I have added the dates from A.D so that it could become easy for the reader to grasp the historical points. As far errors are concerned, I admit the fact that only Prophets are infallibles. Readers are welcomed to point out the mistakes in writing so that they could be removed from the next edition. I don't claim that I am scholar of Islam. I consider myself a student and pray Allah Almighty that my efforts should reach to the public for their wellbeing.

The author of this book is Muhammad Salih bin Ahmad bin Zain Al-Abideen Sheebi. He was born at Makkah in 1854 A.D.(1271 Hijrah). He studied from the scholars of mosque Al Haram. He was the student of Shiekh Abul Khair in Qur'an and Arabic literature.

At the age of 24, he shouldered the responsibility of the key of Ka'aba after his first cousin resigned from the office. He remained in the office till his death. He breathed his last on 10th Zil Hajjah 1334 Hijrah corresponding to 1916 A.D. He was buried in Jannat-ul-Mualla. He visited the capital of Ottoman Empire in 1877 A.D.(1294 Hijrah), 1879 A.D.(1296 Hijrah), 1908 A.D.(1326 Hijrah), and in 1913 A.D.(1332 Hijrah). He was honoured each time with different medals and gifts from the empire. He was very kind and affectionate. Shiekh Muhammad Rashid Raza says "I have never seen a better expert on the history of Quraish other than him".

The author described the history of Quraish under the light of Hadith, Islamic Jurisprudence (fiqh), the book pertaining to Maghazi and books of Seeyar. He used the following books in writing this work.

1.   Fath-ul-Bari by Ibn Hajr Asqalani.

2.   Akhbar-e-Makkah wa maja fiha minul Aasar by Azraqi.

3.   Seerat by Ibn-e-Ishaq

4.   Tafseer by Ibn-e-Katheer

5.   Al-Arjah Al-Miskey wat Tarikh Al Makki by Ali Tabri.

6.   Shifa-ul-Ghuram by Imam Fasi

The purpose of translation of this book is to get the pleasure of Allah Almighty. May Allah accept this effort and forgive my sins and errors. I also request the readers not to forget me and my beloved leader Altaf Bhai in prayers. and supplications.

I am thankful to Senator Nighat Mirza Hina who supported me in compilation of this book. In addition, I am also grateful to S.M. Mahboob-ul-Hassan Bukhari and Hafiz Muhammed Imran Qureshi for providing help in translation and composing. May Allah bless them. I extend my deepest thanks to my friend Sardar Yaseen Malik who bore all the expenditures on this book likewise my other books. I am also thankful to my nephew Abdul Aleem Siddiqui for his unconditional support in this task.

I was entrusted the manuscript of the history of Ka'aba by the family of Sheeba. I transfer all rights of this book to the family of Sheeba. At the end of this translation, reader will find some beautiful pictures of the house of Allah. This is a very important addition in this book. May Allah accept it and forgive us.

Rauf Siddiqui

10th Shawwal, 1429.

10th October, 2008.

Karachi, Pakistan.

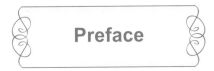

Preface

﴿ اِنَّ اَوَّلَ بَيْتٍ وُّضِعَ لِلنَّاسِ لَلَّذِىْ بِبَكَّةَ مُبَرَكًا وَّ هُدًى لِّلْعٰلَمِيْنَ ۞ فِيْهِ
اٰيٰتٌ بَيِّنٰتٌ مَّقَامُ اِبْرٰهِيْمَ ۚ وَمَنْ دَخَلَهٗ كَانَ اٰمِنًا ﴾

Lo! the first Sanctuary appointed for mankind was that at Becca (Makkah), a blessed place, a guidance to the peoples; [1] Wherein are plain memorials (of Allah's guidance); the place where Abraham stood up to pray; and whoseever entereth it is safe.

A lot of books have been written on the history of Makkah but I have not seen any one on the history of the House of Allah, specifically. The House of Allah and its responsibilities are related to our family in particular and to the Muslims in general. Therefore I have decided to compile a book particularly on the history of Ka'aba. I have tried to see the history of the House of Allah from the Authenticated and unauthenticated hadith. My aim is to write a unique book on the history of Ka'aba. I have taken help from the Tafseer, Hadith, Islamic Jurisprudence (Fiqh), History and books on Seerat. I have chosen authenticated traditions in order to write on the topic. I have named it (Aalamm-ul-Anam Bi Tareekh Baitullah). May Allah lead us on the way of those who are blessed by Allah Almighty and whose works become the ultimate source of inspiration for majority of Muslims.

Muhammad Salih bin Ahmad bin Zainul Abideen Sheebi,
Author

---

[1] Al-i-Imran : 96-97

The Respect for Ka'aba before and after Islam

Ibrahim (blessings of Allah be upon him) constructed Ka'aba with the will of Allah. It was the first ever house on the surface of earth. It became the fountainhead of pure guidance. Allah blessed both the place and its inhabitants. This city came to be known as the city of peace and blessings. Prophet Muhammad (Peace & blessings of Allah be upon him) made Ka'aba the Qibla (Direction of Prayers) for Muslims. From there on it became the center of all religious activities for Muslims who come from all over the world to see the house for seeking the pleasure of Allah. They come here to praise Allah and to worship Him with utmost sincerity. As they do it they are further blessed by the blessings of the Greatest. The pilgrims are chosen by the mercy of Allah and His Benevolence. Allah takes these pilgrims very close to Him the way Allah does with angels when they worship in the Bait-ul-Maamur (the heavenly house of Allah)

Both Christians and Jews worshiped Allah in this Holy house. Both respected the house alike. They would worship in the house besides their mutual differences. They did it for centuries. They used to take asylum in the house if they were afraid. They would not enter until they wore Ahram. Allah almighty got the Makkans realized this blessings in the Holy Qur'an.

﴿ اَوَلَمْ يَرَوْا اَنَّا جَعَلْنَا حَرَمًا اٰمِنًا وَّيُتَخَطَّفُ النَّاسُ مِنْ حَوْلِهِمْ ﴾

Have they not seen that We have appointed a sanctuary immune (from violence), while mankind are ravaged all around them. [1]

This blessing has extended from men to animals and plants. Allah made this house peaceful from the very first day of its creation. Holy Qur'an speaks like this

﴿ فَلْيَعْبُدُوْا رَبَّ هٰذَا الْبَيْتِ ۙ الَّذِيْ اَطْعَمَهُمْ مِّنْ جُوْعٍ ۙ وَّاٰمَنَهُمْ مِّنْ خَوْفٍ ﴾

So let them worship the Lord of this House,
Who hath fed them against hunger.And hath made them safe from fear. [2]

---

[1] Al Ankaboot: 67
[2] Al Quraish: 3,4

Measurements of Ka'aba

The House of Allah is cubic in shape like it was in the era of Holy Prophet Muhammad (peace and blessings of Allah be upon him). It is made of blue stones. It has the height of 15 meters. The wall where Black Stone is kept and its opposite wall each is 10.1 meters high. The wall with a door of Ka'aba in it and its opposite wall has the height of 12 meters each. The Back Stone is at the height of about a meter from ground. The door is 2 meters high. People can ascend by stairs. Ka'aba is located 330 meters above the sea level and is located in the centre of the mosque Al Haram.

If we see the Ka'aba from the door Salam it looked covered with black silk sheet of cloth. The verses of Allah Almighty are written on it. It is tied with a beautiful belt. Qur'anic verses are also imprinted on it with gold and silver. The door of Ka'aba has been painted with silver and gold colours. This door is covered with the sheet of cloth. Qur'anic verses are also imprinted on it.

Maqam-e-Ibrahim [1]. is placed on the right side of Ka'aba. It is like a dome erected on four pillars. The pillars are covered with a cage made of bronze metal. The Stone of Ibrahim (blessings of Allah be upon him) is kept inside it. It is that stone on which Prophet Ibrahim (blessings of Allah be upon him) stood during the construction of the House of Allah. The traces of the feet of Ibrahim (blessings of Allah be upon him) are visible on the stone. It was inside the Ka'aba before the conquest of Makkah. In the era of Umar (Allah be pleased with him) it was transferred to its original place, where it is there since then.

Right behind the Maqam-e-Ibrahim, there is a door of Sheeba. It was the door of mosque Al Haram. If we stand and see to our right, Hateem is visible. Musalla-e-Hanifi is located just behind Hateem.

---

[1] *Maqam-e-Ibrahim is the stone on which Prophet Ibrahim (blessings of Allah be upon him) used to stand during the construction of the Holy Ka'aba. Allah Almighty has ordained Muslims to make it as a place of worship. Qur'an says in Al-Baqara in verse No. 125.*

﴿ وَإِذْ جَعَلْنَا الْبَيْتَ مَثَابَةً لِّلنَّاسِ وَأَمْنًا وَاتَّخِذُوا مِنْ مَّقَامِ إِبْرٰهِمَ مُصَلًّى ط ﴾

And when we made the House (at Mecca) a resort for mankind and a sanctuary, (saying): Take as your place of worship the place where Abraham stood (to pray). And we imposed a duty upon Abraham and Ishmael, (saying): Purify My house for those who go around and those who meditate therein and those who bow down and prostrate themselves (in worship).[2]

---

[2] Al Baqara:125

Famous Constructions of Holy Ka'aba

The following Prophets and eminent persons have constructed or reconstructed the building of Ka'aba, time and again. In either way they had the honour to participate in the establishment of the building of Ka'aba.

1. Adam (blessings of Allah be upon him)

2. Ibrahim and Ismaeel (blessings of Allah be upon them)

3. Quraish

4. Abdullah Ibn-i-Zubair (Allah be pleased with him)

5. Hajjaj bin Yousuf

6. Sultan Murad Khan (IV)

Construction by Adam
(blessing of Allah be upon him)

It is yet to be decided whether Holy Ka'aba was constructed before Adam (blessing of Allah be upon him)? If yes then who did that? The opinions of the historians in this regard are subject to research. Readers must be able to distinguish between authentic and unauthentic ones. Readers are advised to prefer only the authentic and related narrations. A few scholars are of the view that Allah Almighty fixed the place of Ka'aba two thousand years before the creation of the Earth. Allah spread the earth under water.

Adam (blessing of Allah be upon him) was sent to the earth. He experienced the unbearable solitude. He complained Allah about it. Allah sent Baitul Ma'amoor from the heavens. It was the ruby of paradise made up of green emerald doors on eastern and western sides. It was descended at the exact location of the Ka'aba at present. Allah said "O Adam I have descended one house for you. Circumambulate it the way the angels do on the heavens". The Black Stone (Hajr-i-Aswad) was white in the beginning, but by the touches of the impious sinners from among the pilgrims, it became black.

According to a narration, Adam (blessing of Allah be upon him) walked from India to Makkah. Allah sent an angel as a guide to direct him to the House of Allah. Adam (blessing of Allah be upon him) performed pilgrimage. Angels informed him that Allah had accepted his pilgrimage.

Angels said that they had performed pilgrimage two thousand years ago.

Ibn-i-Abbas is reported to have said that Adam (blessings of Allah be upon him) performed pilgrimage forty times. Each time he walked from India to Makkah. At the time of the Tempest of Noah, Ka'aba was lifted to the fourth heaven where the Bait-ul-Maamur is situated. Seventy thousand angels use to circumambulate the house and never get the opportunity to do it again. Gabriel preserved the Black Stone (Hajr-i-Aswad) in the mount of Abu Qabees lest it should be damaged or lost in the Tempest. This place remained empty till the time of Ibrahim (blessings of Allah be upon him).

Ibn-i-Hajr Asqalani reports with reference to Ata that Adam (blessings of Allah be upon him) requested Allah to bless him a house to circumambulate it the way the angels do in the heavens.[1] Allah Almighty says.

$$\text{﴿ وَإِذْ يَرْفَعُ إِبْرَاهِمُ الْقَوَاعِدَ مِنَ الْبَيْتِ وَإِسْمَعِيلُ طَ رَبَّنَا تَقَبَّلْ مِنَّاطِ إِنَّكَ أَنْتَ السَّمِيعُ الْعَلِيمُ ۝ ﴾}$$

And when Abraham and Ishmael were raising the foundations of the House, (Abraham prayed): Our Lord! Accept from us (this duty). Lo! Thou, only Thou, art the Hearer, the Knower. [2]

---

[1] Fath-ul-Bari
[2] Al Baqara: 127

The foundations of the House, according to Ibn-i-Jareer Tabri, mean the foundations of the House of Allah. Scholars have different views about it. Were they raised on the previous foundations or constructed anew by Ibrahim and Ismaeel (blessings of Allah be upon them) [1]. ? According to other scholars, these foundations were laid by Adam (blessings of Allah be upon him). which were lost later. Ata is reported to have said that Adam (blessings of Allah be upon him) said "O Lord I can't hear the angels" Allah replied "you can't because you committed an error. Now go to earth and make a house for me, circumambulate it the way the angles do."

A few scholars are of the view that the foundations of the Ka'aba were laid by the pebbles and stones of the following mountains. They are:

1.   Mount of Hira

2.   Mount of Zeeta

3.   Mount of Seena

4.   Mount of Lebonan

5.   Mount of Joodi

Adam (blessings of Allah be upon him) laid the foundation of the house from the stones of Hira. They were raised by Ibrahim (blessings of Allah be upon him). Mujahid is reported to have said that Ka'aba was

---

[1] Jami-ul-Bayan

made before the creation of this earth and the heavens and was kept on the surface of the water like white foams. The earth was spread under it later on. Similarly Ibn-i-Abbas is reported to have said that the House of Allah was kept on the surface of water two thousand years before the creation of the earth and heavens. The earth was spread under it later on.

Ibn-i-Jareeh is reported to have said that Allah ordered winds to push the water back. The House of Allah appeared like dome. Bait-ul-lah is derived from it. It is also called Umm-ul-Qura.

Ata ibn-e-Rabah reported that the people found a stone on which it was written that I was the lord of Makkah. I had created this house on the same day when I created the moon and the sun.

Imam Neesha Poori narrates in his tafseer from Wahab ibn-i-Munabba that when Adam (blessings of Allah be upon him) came to the earth, he was afraid of his solitude. He asked Allah if He had created anybody who would praise Him. Allah replied I would create people from your offspring who would praise and glorify me. Soon I shall construct a house where people will glorify and worship me. You will make your abode in it. I will specify it for me and shower it with blessings and prefer it to all houses on earth and it will be named my house or House of Allah. My creature will glorify me. I will make it great with my greatness. I will protect it through my sanctity. I shall place it in my

beloved place. I selected this place when I created the earth and the
heavens. I shall make this house peaceful for you and who come after
you. I will purify it and all its surroundings. Whoever respected it has
indeed respected me and whoever treads it down has indeed treads
my sanctity down. Whoever gives amnesty to its inhabitants will be
given amnesty by me. Whoever frightens its inhabitants is disloyal to
me. Whosoever respects it will earn respect by me.

Whosoever disrespects it will be disrespected by me. Residents of it
are my neighbors and protectors of it are my representatives. I have
made it the first house for people and I will protect it by the entities
of heavens and the earth. People will see this house group after group.

$$\text{﴾} وَ اَذِّنْ فِى النَّاسِ بِالْحَجِّ يَأْتُوْكَ رِجَالًا وَّعَلٰى كُلِّ ضَامِرٍ يَّأْتِيْنَ مِنْ كُلِّ فَجٍّ عَمِيْقٍ ۙ ﴿$$

And proclaim unto mankind the Pilgrimage. They will come unto thee
on foot and on every lean camel; they will come from every deep
ravine.[1]

And whoever says takbeer (Allah-o-Akber) and talbeeh (Labbaik
labbaiak Allahuma Labbaik inanl Hamda waniemata laka wal Mulk La
sharika Laka Labbaik) and do umrah for none but me and visit me

---
[1] Al-Hajj: 27

and become my guest and stay with me, I shall cover him with My Mercy. Since It is my Grace and I deserve that.

O Adam, make it abode so long you live, it will settle all Prophets and nations which come after you until it ends on the Prophet Muhammad (peace and blessings of Allah be upon him) He is the final Prophet. I have made him the settler, the resident, the protector and the guardian of this house. He will be honest so long he lives; he will get Me when he demises. I have great reward for him and by that he will have great status by Me. He will be helper. I shall increase the respect and sanctity of this house. I have made it respectful before Muhammad (peace and blessings of Allah be upon him) in your offspring that is Ibrahim (blessings of Allah be upon him). I shall raise the foundations of this house and make it a building and declare the indications of the house of Allah and teach him the commandments of Hajj and set him Imam for the nation who will follow my commandments and enforce them. He will invite the people to My way, I will choose him and show him the righteous path. I shall try him and he will be steadfast, I shall forgive him and he will be thankful to Me. I shall command him and he will follow Me. He will pray Me and I shall accept his prayers in favour of his family and offspring. I shall make him the healer and his descendants the custodian, the protector and the resident of this house. I shall make Ibrahim (blessings of Allah be upon him) Imam of this house and Deen-e-Hanif and all men and Jinn shall follow him.

Ibn Katheer writes that there is no single opinion about who laid first the foundation of Ka'aba. A few cling to the view that angels laid its foundations before Adam (blessings of Allah be upon him). This has been narrated by Imam Baqir, recorded by Imam Qartabi. Imam Abd-ur-Razzaq prefers the narration of Ibni Jareeh in this regard. Still another tradition reveals that Adam (blessings of Allah be upon him) constructed Ka'aba from the stones of five mountains. Their names are:

1. Mount of Hira

2. Mount of Zeeta

3. Mount of Seena

4. Mount of Lebonan

5. Mount of Joodi [1]

Ibne Abbas, Kaab Ahbar, Qutada (Allah be pleased with them) and Wahab bin Munabba narrate that the foundation of the Ka'aba was laid by the Prophet Shees (blessings of Allah be upon him). Most probably these traditions are narrated by the people of book (Ahl-i-Kitab) known as Israeeleiat. These can neither be affirmed nor denied. It is reliable only if it is in consistency with traditions narrated by the Prophet Muhammad (peace and blessings of Allah be upon him).

---

[1] Tafseer Ibn-e-Katheer

History
of Ka'aba

There is a great deal of narrations about the construction of the House of Allah. I have confined myself to the above mentioned traditions. I conclude that the foundations of Ka'aba were laid well before Adam, Ibrahim and Ismaeel (blessings of Allah be upon them). I don't think that Ka'aba was built after Adam (blessings of Allah be upon him) and before Ibrahim (blessings of Allah be upon him) under the light of the traditions. Imam Qastalni reports that the descendents of Adam (blessings of Allah be upon him) constructed it after him. Imam Nasafi, Imam Azrqi, Wahab bin Munabba narrate that the offspring of Adam (blessings of Allah be upon him) constructed the House of Allah after his death. Imam Suhaili writes that the Prophet Shees constructed it. Imam Zarqani cites Ibne Kateer in his Muaata that it is neither reliable that none constructed Ka'aba before Ibrahim (blessings of Allah be upon him) nor he constructed it for the first time. Imam Zarqani narrates from Tabri that Ka'aba was constructed by the angels before Adam (blessings of Allah be upon him). [1]

---

[1] *Sheikh Suleman Jamal writes with reference to Imam Qastalani that the House of Allah was constructed ten times. Firstly by angels secondly by Adam (blessing of Allah be upon him) thirdly by Prophet Shees (blessing of Allah be upon him) fourthly by Ibrahim (blessings of Allah be upon him) fifthly by Emalaqa sixthly by Jarham(name of tribe) seventhly by Qusai eighthly by Quraish in which Holy Prophet Muhammad (peace and blessings of Allah be upon him) had participated ninthly by Abdullah bin Zubair and tenthly by Hajjaj bin Yousuf (Summary from Alfutuhat-ul-Iahia (v:1,p:115,116).*

Imam Baiheqi narrates from Umar (Allah be pleased with him) that

Prophet says when Adam (blessings of Allah be upon him) accomplished

his pilgrimage the angels told him that his pilgrimage had been

accepted.

Wahab bin Munabba reports that Prophet Shees (blessings of Allah

be upon him) constructed it. [1]

---

[1] Dalail-un-Nubuwwa.

Construction of Ka'aba by Ibrahim and Ismaeel
(blessings of Allah be Upon them)

The construction of Ka'aba by Ibrahim and Ismail (blessings of Allah be upon them) is authentically proved through the sources of Qur'an and Ahadith.

Allah Almighty says

وَاِذْ جَعَلْنَا الْبَيْتَ مَثَابَةً لِّلنَّاسِ وَاَمْنًا ۖ وَاتَّخِذُوْا مِنْ مَّقَامِ اِبْرٰهِمَ مُصَلًّى ۖ وَعَهِدْنَآ اِلٰٓى اِبْرٰهِمَ وَاِسْمٰعِيْلَ اَنْ طَهِّرَا بَيْتِيَ لِلطَّآئِفِيْنَ وَالْعٰكِفِيْنَ وَالرُّكَّعِ السُّجُوْدِ ○ وَاِذْ قَالَ اِبْرٰهِمُ رَبِّ اجْعَلْ هٰذَا بَلَدًا اٰمِنًا وَّارْزُقْ اَهْلَهُ مِنَ الثَّمَرٰتِ مَنْ اٰمَنَ مِنْهُمْ بِاللهِ وَالْيَوْمِ الْاٰخِرِ ۖ قَالَ وَمَنْ كَفَرَ فَاُمَتِّعُهُ قَلِيْلًا ثُمَّ اَضْطَرُّهٗ اِلٰى عَذَابِ النَّارِ ۖ وَبِئْسَ الْمَصِيْرُ ○ وَاِذْ يَرْفَعُ اِبْرٰهِمُ الْقَوَاعِدَ مِنَ الْبَيْتِ وَاِسْمٰعِيْلُ ۖ رَبَّنَا تَقَبَّلْ مِنَّا ۖ اِنَّكَ اَنْتَ السَّمِيْعُ الْعَلِيْمُ ○

And when We made the House (at Mecca) a resort for mankind and a sanctuary, (saying): Take as your place of worship the place where Abraham stood (to pray). And we imposed a duty upon Abraham and Ishmael, (saying): Purify My house for those who go around and those who meditate therein and those who bow down and prostrate themselves (in worship).

And when Abraham prayed: My Lord! Make this a region of security
and bestow upon its people fruits, such of them as believe in Allah
and the Last Day, He answered: As for him who disbelieveth, I shall
leave him in contentment for a while, then I shall compel him to the
doom of fire-a hapless journey's end!

And when Abraham and Ishmael were raising the foundations of the
House, (Abraham prayed): Our Lord! Accept from us (this duty). Lo!
Thou, only Thou, art the Hearer, the Knower.[1]

Imam Bukhari is reported to have narrated from Ibne Abbas in his
Saheeh. The summary of which is as follows: Ismaeel[2] was born to
Hajrah (Allah be pleased with her) and Ibrahim (blessings of Allah be
upon him) after 99 years of their marriage by the Will of Allah. Allah
ordained them to go to the barren valley of Makkah. Ibrahim (blessings
of Allah be upon him) left Hajrah (Allah be pleased with her) and infant
Ismaeel there. He gave them some dates and little water. Hajrah (Allah
be pleased with her) inquired Ibrahim (blessings of Allah be upon him)
if it was the order of Allah. He replied her in affirmation. She became
satisfied and remarked that Allah would not ruin us. She came back
to her child Ismaeel. Ibrahim (blessings of Allah be upon him) prayed
Allah.

[1] Al-Baqara : 125,126,127
[2] Ismaeel (blessings of Allah be upon him), the eldest son of Ibrahim (blessings of Allah
be upon him), was first married to a lady from Jarham tribe. His second wife
Syeda Bint-e-Madaad gave birth to his 12 sons. (Tareekh-e-Tibri)

﴿رَبَّنَآ اِنِّيْٓ اَسْكَنْتُ مِنْ ذُرِّيَّتِيْ بِوَادٍ غَيْرِ ذِيْ زَرْعٍ عِنْدَ بَيْتِكَ الْمُحَرَّمِ ۙ رَبَّنَا لِيُقِيْمُوا الصَّلٰوةَ فَاجْعَلْ اَفْئِدَةً مِّنَ النَّاسِ تَهْوِيْٓ اِلَيْهِمْ وَارْزُقْهُمْ مِّنَ الثَّمَرٰتِ لَعَلَّهُمْ يَشْكُرُوْنَ ٠﴾

Our Lord! Lo! I have settled some of my posterity in an uncultivable valley near unto Thy Holy House, our Lord! that they may establish proper worship; so incline some hearts of men that they may yearn toward them, and provide Thou them with fruits in order that they may be thankful.[1]

When dates and water were over and Ismaeel needed water she tried to fetch water from the mountain Safa. She did not see anyone there to provide water. She came down to see her child lest he should be harmed. In that she mounted and came down from the mountain Safa seven times. Ibne Abbas says this is the reason why people do Saee (running in between the two mountains Safa and Marwa as a ritual made compulsory by Allah). When she mounted Marwa for the last time she heard a voice and halted to listen. An angel beats his wings and water springs from the earth. She took some water from it and it continued. Angel said that O Hajrah (Allah be pleased with her) don't fear here is the House of Allah. Your son and his father will construct it. Allah will not waste people around it. [2]

---

[1] Al-Ibrahim (blessings of Allah be upon him): 37
[2] Sahi Bukhari

This tradition shows on the one hand that Ismaeel (blessings of Allah be upon him) was brought up in Makkah and on the other that he constructed Ka'aba. This was the purpose to describe the tradition. This tradition also indicates that the House of Allah was on a small but high mountain before the construction by Ibrahim and Ismail (blessings of Allah be upon them). Later Ibrahim and Ismaeel (blessings of Allah be upon them) constructed it by the pebbles and stones. We get many traditions in this regard.

The historian Ibne Jareer writes with reference to Mujahid and others that when Allah ordained Ibrahim (blessings of Allah be upon him) to settle in the House of Allah he left for it with his family Hajrah (Allah be pleased with her) and little son Ismaeel. Ibne Jareer writes that they rode on Burraq which is as fast as lightning.

Gibreel (blessings of Allah be upon him) accompanied them so that he could direct them to the House of Allah. On the way Ibrahim (blessings of Allah be upon him) asked Gibreel (blessings of Allah be upon him) "is it the place where I am ordained to stay?" He replied every time "further" till they reached Makkah. He saw the nation of Emalqa around Makkah.

The house of Allah was, then, like a round and Red Mountain. Ibrahim (blessings of Allah be upon him) inquired again "is it the place where I am commanded to leave my family?" Gibreel (blessings of Allah be upon him) said, "Yes". Ibrahim (blessings of Allah be upon him) took his wife Hajrah (Allah be pleased with her) and son Ismaeel to the Black Stone (Hajar-e-Aswad) and asked Hajrah (Allah be pleased with her) to make a hut there.as Allah Almighty says

﴿رَبَّنَآ اِنِّيْٓ اَسْكَنْتُ مِنْ ذُرِّيَّتِيْ بِوَادٍ غَيْرِ ذِيْ زَرْعٍ عِنْدَ بَيْتِكَ الْمُحَرَّمِ ۙ رَبَّنَا لِيُقِيْمُوا الصَّلٰوةَ فَاجْعَلْ اَفْئِدَةً مِّنَ النَّاسِ تَهْوِيْٓ اِلَيْهِمْ وَارْزُقْهُمْ مِّنَ الثَّمَرٰتِ لَعَلَّهُمْ يَشْكُرُوْنَ ٠﴾

Our Lord! Lo! I have settled some of my posterity in an uncultivable valley near unto Thy Holy House, our Lord! that they may establish proper worship; so incline some hearts of men that they may yearn toward them, and provide Thou them with fruits in order that they may be thankful.[1]

---

[1] Al-Ibrahim: 37

Ibne Hameed says when Ibrahim (blessings of Allah be upon him) along with his family reached Makkah; an angel came to Hajrah (Allah be pleased with her) and indicated to her the place of Ka'aba. The House of Allah was round and Red Mountain. He said to both of them: this is the first house ever constructed on the face of earth. This is Baitullah Al-Ateeq. Let it be known that Ibrahim and Ismaeel (blessings of Allah be upon them) will raise its foundations. (Allah knows the best)

Ibne Jareer Tabri, the historian, says "To me personally the saying of Allah in the Holy Qur'an is the most authentic in which He says that Ibrahim and Ismaeel (blessings of Allah be upon them) will raise its foundations."

It is correct that these foundations are the same as set by Adam and he had placed them in Baithullah. It is the same dome said by Ata. He says that it was made up with the foams of water by Allah. It is the same pearl or emerald descended from heavens. It is that foundation laid by Adam (blessings of Allah be upon him) but fell and raised again by Ibrahim and Ismaeel (blessings of Allah be upon them).

We can not say anything definite on the issue because reality can only be unlocked by the words of Allah and the sayings of Holy Prophet Muhammad (peace and blessings of Allah be upon him).

Allah says

وَإِذْ يَرْفَعُ إِبْرَاهِمُ الْقَوَاعِدَ مِنَ الْبَيْتِ وَإِسْمَاعِيْلُ رَبَّنَا تَقَبَّلُ مِنَّا إِنَّكَ
أَنْتَ السَّمِيعُ الْعَلِيْمُ ○

And when Abraham and Ishmael were raising the foundations of the
House, (Abraham prayed): Our Lord! Accept from us (this duty). Lo!
Thou, only Thou, art the Hearer, the Knower .[1]

Imam Qastalni says that this verse indicates that the foundations of
the house were already laid before Ibrahim (blessings of Allah be upon
him). Imam Razi writes that Bait-ullah was present at the time of Adam
(blessings of Allah be upon him). This is the correct view.[2] This was
strengthened by Ibne Jareer Tabri. He says that the foundations of
Ka'aba were already there. Ibrahim and Ismaeel (blessings of Allah
be upon them) raised the foundations of the seventh earth.
Saeed bin jubair reports from Abbas (Allah be pleased with him) that
the foundations they raised were already there.

Ata says that Adam (blessings of Allah be upon him) complained that
I can't hear the angels. Allah said "O Adam I sent one house for you.
Circumambulate it the way it is done on heavens".

---

[1] Al-Baqara: 127
[2] Tafseer Al Kabeer

Measurement:

According to a tradition, Ibrahim (blessings of Allah be upon him) had raised the foundations of Ka'aba already set by Adam (blessings of Allah be upon him). He kept its height 9 yards (old times) and its circumference 13 yards. Another tradition says that Allah sent revelation to Ibrahim (blessings of Allah be upon him) to follow Sakeena. This Sakeena had circled the Ka'aba. Both of them started digging to uncover the foundations set by Adam (blessings of Allah be upon him).

Imam Tabri and Hakim Ali narrate from Ali that Ibrahim (blessings of Allah be upon him) had seen something like a cloud shadowing on the place of Bait-ullah. It addressed him "O Ibrahim (blessings of Allah be upon him) construct Ka'aba under the shadow. Don't increase or decrease it."

Similarly Allah Almighty says in Holy Qur'an :

$$
\text{﴾ وَاِذْ بَوَّأْنَا لِاِبْرٰهِيْمَ مَكَانَ الْبَيْتِ اَنْ لَّا تُشْرِكْ بِيْ شَيْئًا وَّطَهِّرْ بَيْتِيَ لِلطَّآئِفِيْنَ وَالْقَآئِمِيْنَ وَالرُّكَّعِ السُّجُوْدِ ۝ ﴿}
$$

And (remember) when We prepared for Abraham the place of the (Holy) House, saying: Ascribe thou nothing as partner unto Me, and purify My House for those who make the round (thereof) and those who stand and those who bow and make prostration.[1]

Maqam-e-Ibrahim (Place of Ibrahim):

It is well known that it is that stone which was brought by Ismaeel (blessings of Allah be upon him) for his father so that Ibrahim (blessings of Allah be upon him) could stand on it to help his son to raise the foundations of the House of Allah. Consequently the work was accomplished.

Ibn Hajr Asqalani interprets that the stone brought by Ismaeel (blessings of Allah be upon him) is the Maqam-e-Ibrahim. Ibrahim bin Nafie narrates when Ibrahim (blessings of Allah be upon him) raised the foundations of the Holy Ka'aba, he got tired. He was unable to lift the stones. Then he stood on the Maqam-i-Ibrahim. [2]

When the task was over, Gibreel (blessings of Allah be upon him) came to Ibrahim (blessings of Allah be upon him) and taught the rites of pilgrimage. Ibrahim (blessings of Allah be upon him) stood on the Maqam-e-Ibrahim and said "O mankind answer the call of Allah". Both of them stood on their place meanwhile

---

[1] Al-Hajj: 26
[2] Fath-ul-Bari

Ishaq and Sara (blessings of Allah be upon them) came from Jerusalam and performed pilgrimage. Ibrahim (blessings of Allah be upon him) went back to Syria and passed away there. Imam Fakihi reports with reference to Mujahid from Ibne Abbas that Ibrahim (blessings of Allah be upon him) stood on this stone and said "O people pilgrimage has been made compulsory on you". This call was heared by every man and woman even the children in the wombs of women and backs of men. Every believer and those who would do Hajj till the day of Judgment replied "O Allah I am present O Allah I am present."

Abu Juham narrates when Ismaeel (blessings of Allah be upon him) went in the valley to search a stone, Gibreel (blessings of Allah be upon him) came down with the Black Stone (Hajar-e-Aswad). Remember the Black Stone (Hajar-e-Aswad) was lifted to the heavens at the time of the Tempest of Noah. When Ismaeel (blessings of Allah be upon him) inquired where it came from and who brought it, Ibrahim (blessings of Allah be upon him) replied him he who did not hand me over to you and your stone.

Ibne Abi Hatim reports with reference to Sadi that this stone was brought from India. It was like Sughama. Imam Fakihi narrates with reference to Ibne Abbas that by Allah they have neither constructed the house with clay and lime nor they had the servants to construct the roof of it. Ali (Allah be pleased with him) reports that they used to construct it according to Saq. Abdullah bin amr bin Aas (Allah be pleased with him) reports that they took stones and pebbles from the following mountains to construct the Ka'aba.

1.   Mount of Hira

2.   Mount of Sabir

3.   Mount of Toor

4.   Mount of Lebonan

5.   Mount of Khamar means Mount of Bait-ul-Maqdis.

Ibne Jareeh narrates a tradition recorded by Imam Abd-ur-Razzaq in his Musannaf. Adam (blessing of Allah be upon him) took stones from the folowing five mountains.

1.   Mount of Hira

2.   Mount of Zeeta

3.   Mount of Seena

4.   Mount of Lebonan

5.   Mount of Joodi.

Muhammad bin Talha narrates that I have heard that the foundations of Ka'aba were laid by the stones from the six mountains. They are: Mount of Abu Qabees, Mount of Quds, Mount of Warqan, Mount of Rizwi, Mount of Ahad, Mount of Toor.

Summary:

Ibrahim and Ismaeel (blessings of Allah be upon them) laid the foundations of the Holy Ka'aba on an elevated mountain by the will of Allah. Ibrahim (blessings of Allah be upon him) was constructing and Ismaeel (blessings of Allah be upon him) was bringing the stones. Ibrahim (blessings of Allah be upon him) joined the stones together to erect its walls. He ordered his son Ismaeel (blessings of Allah be upon him) to bring him a stone on which he could stand and erect the walls of the building. Gibreel (blessings of Allah be upon him) came with the Black Stone and Ismaeel (blessings of Allah be upon him) placed it there. Ibrahim (blessings of Allah be upon him) raised the walls of Ka'aba further upto nine yards and compound thirty yards (olden times). Hateem was incorporated in it. It had no roof. He made one door and dug a pit close to it so that people may drop their gifts in it.

The building of Ka'aba was made for the sole purpose of worship of Allah. It has been authenticated that Ibrahim and Ismaeel (blessings of Allah be upon them) had constructed the Ka'aba. This is quite evident in the Holy Qur'an. There is a possibility that Maqam-i-Ibrahim might be the place of prayer and worship of Prophet Ibrahim (blessings of Allah be upon him). This view point is narrated by the Arabs with consensus. The other possibility is that it was the place on which Ibrahim (blessings of Allah be upon him) stood and constructed the Ka'aba as given by the traditions we have mentioned above. Imam Fakharuddin Razi writes that Maqam-i-Ibrahim comprises a lot of signs. It has preserved the footmarks of Ibrahim (blessings of Allah be upon him) although it was as hard as rock. It has remained as a souvenir up till now though the signs of other Prophets have been lost. It is still another special sign of prophet Ibrahim. (blessings of Allah be upon him) This sign has been protected by Allah from the Jews, Christians and infidels which is yet another indication. Hence it is proved that it has a lot of indications of Allah, the great. It is said that Prophet Muhammad (peace and blessings of Allah be upon him) or Umar Farooq (Allah be pleased with him) changed its position.[1]

---

[1] Tafseer Ibn-e-Kabeer

Construction of Ka'aba by Quraish

Ka'aba was demolished many times after the construction of Ibrahim and Ismaeel (blessings of Allah be upon them) According to the historians, it was demolished and reconstructed 35 times. According to my research it was reconstructed twice after Ibrahim and Ismaeel (blessings of Allah be upon them). First by Emaliqa which was followed by Jarham as Ibn Hajar Asqalani reports with reference to Ishaq bin Rahweeh that after Ibrahim's (blessings of Allah be upon him) construction it was demolished and reconstructed by Emaliqa. It was followed by Jarham. Later it was reconstructed by the Quraish. There were many reasons to reconstruct the Ka'aba. Fakehi with reference to Abdulllah bin Umar (Allah be pleased with him) reports that the walls of Ka'aba were more higher than the average height of a man.

They decided to increase its height further and cover it with a roof. Yaqoob bin Sufyan with reference to Zuhri reports that once a lady burned charcoal in the house of Allah. Its sparks burnt the curtains of the Ka'aba. Imam Hakim and Tabrani say that at the time of ignorance the building of Ka'aba was constructed with big stones without using any lime. Its height was up to a camel's neck. The building of the Ka'aba used to be covered by a sheet of cloth in the circular shape. A ship from Rome was broken down at the beach of Jeddah. Quraish rushed to the spot to get its wood. They met there with a Roman carpenter. They brought both the carpenter and the wood with them to Makkah. Whenever they decided to reconstruct Ka'aba, a serpent would threaten them. Then a serpent eater bird was sent by Allah who had thrown the serpent away at Ajyad. Quraish demolished the building in order to reconstruct it with the help of the stones of the valley. Imam Bukhari, Imam Muslim, and Ibn-i-Maja report with reference to Aisha (Allah be pleased with her) about the construction of the building. She said I inquired Prophet if Hateem was the part of the Ka'aba. Holy Prophet Muhammad (peace and blessings of Allah be upon him) replied me in affirmative.

She inquired again why the people did not include it in Baitullah. Prophet said they did not have enough funds for that. "Then why did they increase the height of the door of Ka'aba", she inquired.

"They did it so that they could use their discretionary powers to permit or stop people to enter the sacred place", Prophet replied. Holy Prophet further said if he would not have been afraid of their ignorance and opposition, he would have included Hateem in the Ka'aba and would have shortened the height of its doors.[1]

Imam Termizi and Imam Nasai (Allah be pleased with them) report that Aisha (Allah be pleased with her) expressed her wish to offer prayer in the Ka'aba but Prophet took her hand and asked her to offer it in Hateem. He said it is also the part of Ka'aba. Your nation detached it from Ka'aba during constructions.[2]

Hence the above mentioned traditions show that their constructed building has remained intact upto our time without any change.

Characteristics of their reconstruction

An authentic tradition about the reconstruction of Ka'aba says that when Ka'aba was burnt, Quraish decided to demolish it. Walid bin Mugheera Makhzoomi said that Allah does not destroy those who want to restore the Ka'aba in order. He along with Abbas (Allah be pleased with him) mounted the roof of Ka'aba and said "O Allah we want to reconstruct it".

---

[1] Sahih Bukhari
[2] Jam-e-Termizi

Then he started demolishing it. People did not see him being cursed by Allah. They started helping him in the work. They decided to increase its height further and cover it with a new roof,since someone had stolen the money from inside due to the low height of walls. It was decided that two men from each tribe will bring the stones to build it.

Our Holy Prophet Muhammad (peace and blessings of Allah be upon him) and his uncle used to bring stones from the place Ajyad. When the work reached upto the fixation of the Black Stone, a controversy erupted. Finally it was decided that whoever enters first in the courtyard of Holy Ka'aba will fix the Black Stone. By the blessings of Allah, it was Muhammad (peace and blessings of Allah be upon him). He asked them to bring a sheet of cloth and place the Black Stone on it. He asked every tribe leader to hold the corner of the sheet carrying it upto its place. Prophet then affixed it himself. Ishaq bin Rahweeh narrates a tradition about the reconstruction work of Ibrahim (blessings of Allah be upon him). When Quraish reconstructed it after Jarham, Holy Prophet was young at that time. When the time came to fix the Black Stone, a controversy arose. It was decided that whoever will come first from this street will decide the matter. Holy Prophet (peace & blessings of Allah be upon him) came and asked to bring a sheet of cloth and place the Black Stone on it. Leader of every tribe was told to hold the corner of the cloth.

Ibn-i-Hajarah Asqalani and Dawood Tayalsi say about this tradition that Quraish decided that whoever entered from the door of Bani Shaiba shall decide the matter. Prophet entered the gate first and was informed about the problem. A piece of cloth was brought to him. He placed the Black Stone on it. Every member was invited to hold the corner of the sheet. When they reached up to the proper place, Prophet himself placed it. Imam Fakehi says that Umaya, the brother of Waild bin Mugheera Makhzoomi advised that whoever enters first the building of Ka'aba would decide the matter. It was Walid bin Mugheera Makhzoomi who indicated it first according to the narration of Musa bin Uqba. He who forbad Quraish to spend any impure money in the reconstruction, Ibn-i-Ishaq reports, it was none other than Wahab bin Umr bin Amir bin Imran bin Makhzoom.

Summary:

Hafiz Ibne Katheer writes with reference to Ibne Ishaq that Muhammad bin Ishaq bin yasar writes in his classical biography on the life of Prophet Muhammad (peace & blessings of Allah be upon him) that when Prophet reached up to the age of thirty five, Quraish were gathered to construct the building of Ka'aba. The height of Ka'aba was more heigher than the average height of a man. They decided to further raise the height of walls and construct the roof over it because somebody had stolen the treasure from the hidden pit of Ka'aba.

The stolen money was found with a man Dweek who belonged to the tribe of Khuzaa. The Quraish cut his hand in punishment According to some other views thief left the money with him (Dweek). When a Roman ship was broken down at Jeddah port, Quraish managed to get the wood from the ship and successfully convinced a Roman merchant to prepare the roof for the House of Allah. A carpenter from Qibt was hired by the Quraish. The offerings in the treasure-pit where all gifts and donations where kept, naturally attracted a huge serpent to make it its abode. The serpent used to creep from time to time to the top of the pit, naturally causing terror. One day a serpent eater secretary bird appeared and making a dart, captured the serpent and flew away. It was great rejoicing for the people of Makkah. It was announced that only pure money should be offered for the sacred building. Impure and usurious peoples were asked not to contribute anything. Nor earnings through atrocities and by unfair means were acceptable. Ishaq says that some people attributed it to Walid bin Mugheera bin Amr bin Makhzoom. The work of the construction was distributed. The responsibility for door was given to the tribes Bani Abd Manaf and Zuhra , the responsibility of Hajarah - i-Aswad and Rukn-i-Yamani was assigned to Bani Makhzoom and Quraish . Similarly the external work of Ka'aba was given to the tribes of Bani Jamaa and Saham. The work of Hateem was given to the tribe of Bani Abd-id-Dar bin Qusai, Bani Asad bin Abdul Aza bin Qusai,and Bani Adi bin Kaab bin Loi.

When they were about to demolish the damaged building, Walid bin Mugheera said that he would do it first and said "O Allah We want good" and started demolishing it from both sides of the building. On that night people stopped working and said, " if any curse comes to us we will not advance further. We should reconstruct the already demolished part provided any curse doses not come to us which means Allah Almighty is happy with us". In the morning Walid started his work. The people, after observing him uncursed started helping him.They dug until they have found the basis of Ka'aba laid by Ibrahim (blessings of Allah be upon him). It was a stone, green in color. According to my narration when a member of demolishing party tried to uproof that stone of foundation, the whole Makkah started shaking. They stopped working. According to Ibn-i-Ishaq, the tribes of Quraish then collected the stones and pebbles and started construction of Ka'aba till they reached to the fixation of the Black Stone. Here erupted a controversy. Each tribe wished to take the honor to its tribe. They were at the brink of a bloodshed. Banu Abd made a pact with banu Aadi bin Kaab bin L'oi. A cup of blood was brought and both tribes soaked their hands. This is known as Laaqatdum. Quraish remained in this state for four to five days. Then they gathered in the mosque and consulted each other. A tradition says that Umayyah bin Mugheerah bin Abdullah bin Amr bin Makhzoom who was the oldest among the Quraish, declared that "who would enter first should decide the matter"

Quraish agreed. By the grace of Allah Prophet Muhammad (peace & blessings of Allah be upon him) entered first. The Quraish shouted "The trust-worthy has come we are ready to make him the judge. He is Muhammad." Holy Prophet Muhammad (peace & blessings of Allah be upon him) affixed the Black Stone with his own hands. After the leader of each tribe held all the corners of the sheet and lifted it collectively until they reached the place. The remaining construction was accomplished. Quraish used to call Prophet Muhammad (peace & blessings of Allah be upon him) Ameen (the honest) much before the attainment of Prophethood. Ibn-e-Ishaq says that the height of Ka'aba was eighteen yards. The curtain of Ka'aba was made of kitaan. Later on it used to be covered by woolen cloth. Ka'aba was covered with Deebaj by Hajjaj. Hafiz Ibne Katheer writes that this construction lasted until Abdullah bin Zubair reconstructed it again.

Construction Of Ka'aba
by Abdullah bin Zubair

Imam Bukhari narrates with reference to Ayesha (Allah be pleased with her) that Prophet Muhammad (peace & blessings of Allah be upon him) said if your nation would not have been closed to the days of ignorance, I would have ordered to demolish Ka'aba and include the detached part in it upto the ground. I would have made the eastern and western doors and reconstruct it up to the foundation laid by Ibrahim (blessing of Allah be upon him). This induced Abdullah bin Zubiar (Allah be pleased with him) to demolish Ka'aba and reconstruct it.[1]

Yazeed says I saw Abdullah bin Zubair (Allah be pleased with him) demolishing and reconstructing and affixing the Black Stone.I saw the foundation laid by Ibrahim (blessing of Allah be upon him).They were like the humps of camel. Jareer says I inquired the exect location of the foundation. He replied "let me show you" I went along with him, he indicated towards the stone. Jareer says it was about six yards in length. Imam Muslim narrates that when Ka'aba was burnt in the epoch of Yazeed bin Muaawia, the people of Syria damaged the Ka'aba.Abdulah bin Zubair waited till the season of Hajj so that he

---

[1] Sahih Bukhari

could provoke the people of Syria to wage war against the regime. When people saw the damaged Ka'aba he asked if he should reconstruct it or repair the damaged parts.

Ibne Abbas advised him that he should repair the damage parts and Baitullah should remain the same as it was at the time people embraced Islam. Its stones should be unchanged as they were at the advent of Prophet Muhammad (peace & blessings of Allah be upon him). Abdullah bin Zubair (Allah be pleased with him) remarked "if your house is burnt would you not reconstruct it? What do you think of the House of Allah? I took Istikhara (seeking Allah's consent) thrice". When he decided to demolish the buildings people worried that some calamity might be inflicted by Allah Almighty. One man mounted on the roof of Ka'aba and threw a stone when people saw the man not been cursed they started demolishing the impaired building of Ka'aba. Abdullah bin Zubair (Allah be pleased with him) made the pillars until the building was erected. Abdullah bin Zubair (Allah be pleased with him) narrates from Ayesha (Allah be pleased with her) to have listened from Prophet Muhammad (peace & blessings of Allah be upon him) saying if people were not close to the ignorance and had enough money I would have constructed and included Hateem in the House of Allah. I would have made the entrance and exit gates. Abdullah bin Zubair (Allah be pleased with him) said " Today I have enough money to reconstruct the House of Allah. I am not afraid of people any more." Abdullah bin Zubair (Allah be pleased with him) said "today I have enough money and I am not afraid that the people would go astray". Then he dug the earth five yards deep and reached upto the basis laid by Ibrahim (blessings of Allah be upon him). People were shown the basis. Abdullah bin Zubair (Allah be pleased with him) reconstructed Ka'aba on these foundations. Ka'aba had the height of eighteen yards. Abdullah bin Zubair (Allah be pleased with him) further increased its height by ten yards and made two doors one to enter and the other to exit. When he was martyred, Hajaj told Abdul Malik bin Marwan that Abdullah bin Zubair (Allah be pleased with him) had reconstructed the building of Ka'aba on the foundations of Ibrahim (blessings of Allah be upon him). The people of Makkah had the honor to see the foundations laid by Ibrahim (blessings of Allah be upon him). Abdul Malik replied to Hajjaj that Abdullah bin Zubair (Allah be pleased with him) did something irrational. He ordered to demolish Hateem and keep the increased height of Ka'aba. He further ordered to remove the door which was introduced by Abdullah bin Zubair (Allah be pleased with him). Hajjaj demolished the building and removed the second door. Ibn-i- Hajr cites many traditions in Fath-ul-Bari. I am mentioning just a few. He says that Imam Fakehe narrates when the people of Syria burnt Ka'aba and stoned it through Minjiq (a heavy manual machine on wheels to throw heavy stones) the building of Ka'aba was demolished.

Ibn-i-Saad writes in his book, 'Tabqaat' that when Yazid bin Muawiya's Commander Hussain bin Amr received the news of the death of Yazid in 684 A.D. (65 Hijrah), he decamped and left the place. Another tradition goes with reference to Waqadi in which he refutes that Abdullah bin Zubair (Allah be please with him) constructed Ka'aba in 65 hijra (684 A.D.). He said according to me it is more authentic that the building of Ka'aba was constructed after seventy days the Syrians left. Azraqi favored this opinion. This event took place on fifteen Jamadiusani 64 hijra (683 A.D.). Ibn-i-Hajr brings harmony in these traditions by saying that Abdullah bin Zubair (Allah be pleased with him) started construction which was prolonged till the Hajj season so that the people could go against Bani Umayya.[1] Tabri adds that this event took place in the month of Rajab. Imam Muslim narrates with reference to Ata that Ibn-i-Abbas forbad but Abdullah bin Zubair (Allah be pleased with him) replied if your house is burnt will you not reconstruct it? I consulted Allah almighty (Istakhara) thrice. He decided to destroy the building. People kept on abstaining him from it. One man reached on the top of Ka'aba and threw a stone. When people observed him not being cursed by Allah, they followed Abdullah bin Zubair (Allah be pleased with him) to demolish the building. Abdullah bin Zubair (Allah be pleased with him) made the pillars. The building was demolished and its foundation was raised.

Ibne Aaina narrates with reference to Mujahid that we went to Mina to wait for the curse. They waited there for three days for the punishment. Abdullah bin Zubair (Allah be please with him) climbed on the walls of Ka'aba to demolish it.

Another tradition say that all useable things were again hanged and placed and unuseful things were buried in the Ka'aba. He was failed to discover the foundations laid by Ibrahim (blessings of Allah be upon him). He tried hard to get there and finally his efforts were fruitful and reached the basis laid by Ibrahim (blessings of Allah be upon him). He found the basis as hard as rock (like the head of camel). He found them well integrated and strong. He praised and glorified Allah. He invited people to show these foundations and kept them as evidence. Ata's tradition shows that Ka'aba's height was 18 yards. Azraqi supported him and said that Abdullah bin Zubair (Allah be pleased with him) increased 9 yards further. Ibn Hajr says that all the traditions show the fact that Quraish left the basis of Ibrahim (blessings of Allah be upon him) and Abdullah bin Zubair reconstructed on the Ibrahimic basis. Hajaj reconstructed on the tradition of Quraish (not Ibrahimic)

Completion of
Construction of Ka'aba

Ibni Abdullah, Qazi Ayyaz and others narrate when Mansoor intended

to build Ka'aba like that of Abdullah bin Zubair (Allah be pleased with

him), Malik forbade him. He remarked if it is allowed, Ka'aba would

become a playful object in the hands of the kings.

bin Hajr writes Abdullah Ibn Abbas (Allah be pleased with him). was

too worried for the same reason. He indicated Abdullah bin Zubair

(Allah be pleased with him) about it and asked him to repair the building

of Ka'aba rather than reconstructing it. Following his beloved Prophet

he said I am afraid that the kings after you would change it. According

to the tradition of Azraqi, Sulaiman bin Abdul Malik intended to

reconstruct the demolished part of the building but he did not go for

it after he came to know that Hajjaj demolished it on the orders of his

father Abdul Malik. We don't find any evidence in the history that

anybody changed the construction of Hajjaj. Though some changes

have been made recently in the Meezab-i-Rehmat and its door. Similarly

some changes have been brought in the walls, roof and stairs. They

were marbled.

Azraqi with reference to bin Jarih writes that Walid bin Abdul Malik

was the first who marbled the floor. These changes were made in the

wall in 883 A.D. (270 Hijrah). Further alterations came in 1147 A.D.(542

Hijrah), 1222 A.D. (619 Hijrah), 1281 A.D. (680 Hijrah), 1411 A.D.

(814 Hijrah) respectively. In our era Sultan Malik Mueed brought some

alterations in Meezab-i-Rehmat. Ayash bin Abi Rabia Makhzoomi

narrates that so long people keep the honor of Ka'aba; they will live

a life full of peace and tranquility. If they go the other way round, they

would be perished. This tradition was narrated by Imam Ahmad, bin

Majah and Umr bin Shiba.

Construction by Hajjaj bin Yousuf

Sahih (authentic) traditions show that Hajjaj did not demolish Ka'aba completely. He only removed the area increased by Abdullah bin Zubair (Allah be pleased with him) in Hateem and returned the Ka'aba to its original position where it was at the time of Prophet Muhammad (peace and blessings of Allah be upon him). Muslim records a tradition when Abdullah bin Zubair (Allah be pleased with him) was martyred, Hajjaj wrote a letter to Abdul Malik that Abdullah bin Zubair (Allah be pleased with him) reconstructed the Ka'aba on the foundations of Ibrahim (blessings of Allah be upon him). He replied that we would not consider the nonsense of Abdullah bin Zubair (Allah be pleased with him). However the increased height should be kept as it is. Remove the door introduced by Abdullah bin Zubair (Allah be pleased with him) and exclude the Hateem. Hajjaj followed the decrees. bin Hajr concludes that so far I have collected the traditions indicate the fact that Abdullah bin Zubair (Allah be pleased with him) made a door which required another gate on the opposite side. Azraqi records a tradition that Hajjaj brought changes in the walls of Hateem and in the door along with the doorsill at the right side which had the height of about four yards. Fakehi writes in Akhbar-i-Makkah that he observed the closed door from the inside door of Ka'aba which was similar to the original door in width and height.

Imam Shafiee (Allah be pleased with him) writes in his well known

Kitab-ul-Aam that Quraish did not reach upto the foundations laid by

Ibrahim (blessings of Allah be upon him) and excluded Hateem from

Ka'aba. Abdullah bin Zubair (Allah be pleased with him) reconstructed

the building on Ibrahimic basis. Hajjaj changed it again. A few kings

wanted to bring the building of Ka'aba back on the Ibrahimic basis but

some people disliked it. They had shown reservations in this regard.

It was necessary so that the Ka'aba should not become a playful thing

in their hands. It should be protected from the wants and lusts of the

people. Prophet Muhammad (peace and blessings of Allah be upon

him) kept it as it was. Similarly righteous caliphs followed the footsteps

of their beloved Prophet. I did not find any evidence in the history that

after Abdullah bin Zubair (Allah be pleased with him) anybody brought

major changes in the building of Ka'aba except a few alterations made

by Abasides and Al-i-Usman.

Construction by Sultan Murad Khan the IV

Heavy rain fell in the epoch of Sultan Murad Khan, started on Wednesday of 14th Shaban in between the Zuhr and Asr and continued till the night of Thursday which resulted in disastrous flood. The mosque Al-Haram was flooded with water.

The flood water entered the Ka'aba and reached upto the half hieght of the walls. Many important people of that time died in this disastrous flood. The Syrian wall, eastern and western walls fell. Sorrow spreaded everywhere. The head of Makkah Masood bin Idrees bin Hassan lighted the lights inside the mosque Al-Haram who was the holder of the key of Ka'aba. The key holder of the Ka'aba Muhammad JamaludDin Qasim Shaibi entered the Ka'aba and brought qindeel from his house to protect them. Next day, it was Friday. Ameer of Makkah and some other resposibile people gathered.

The people cleaned the mosque Al Haram. Imam led the prayer and re-established the rites of Baitullah. The people gathered the fallen stones of the building and deposited them at the Maqam Hanafi. Some other stones were deposited near door of Salam. A delegation was sent along with a letter containing the decree to the minister of Makkah to inform him about the catastrophy and to inform the Sultan about it. This delegation went to Egypt by the end of month of Shabaan.

Ameer of Ka'aba ordered engineers to clean the compound. The original door of Ka'aba was replaced by a wooden door from Jeddah. A wooden partition was made to protect people from the construction inconveniences. This took place in the month of Ramadan. All the wooden walls were made in the month of Shawwal. The Ameer of Makkah covered the Ka'aba with green sheet and offered prayer and made seven ritual circumambulations on the third day of Shawwal in 1629 A.D. (1039) Hijrah. The delegation returned back from Egypt. Agha Rizwan, an expert engineer, came with the royal orders on 17th Shawwal to Ameer of Makkah. He also brought with him the Khaqani clothes as a gift. A meeting was held on the issue. Later he started his work and accomplished it before the arrival of pilgrims.

Syed Muhammad Afindi, an assistant engineer came to Makkah by sea on 16th Rabi-us-Sani 1630 A.D. (1040 Hijra). He came to assist the engineer in the work. He, too, came with another Usmani Khilat as a gift to the Ameer-i-Makkah. Shiekh of Haram Syed Abdul Karim bin Idrees, engineer Agha Rizwan Bak, assistant engineer Syed Muhammad Afindi, and other scholars met in Hateem.

They met Ameer of Makkah with a robe of honor. He was having a walk in his garden advised by doctor. He wore up the dress immediately. He passed away on 10th Rabiussani on Tuesday. Sharif bin Abdullah bin Hassan bin Ubai Nami, Syed Muhammad Afindi and Shiekh of Haram Attaqi Afindi arrived and presented engineers the robes of honor to them on 13th Jumadi-ul-Awwal on Saturday.

Syed Muhammad Afindi asked the opinion of all the scholars if a sheet is hanged on the Ka'aba so that people could work behind it. A few favored it while others disagreed. On 17th Jumadi-ul-Awwal on Friday, Ameer of Makkah Sharif bin Abdullah bin Hassan along with Sadat (sayyeds) and scholars met in the Hateem. They debated on demolishing the walls of Ka'aba. The Sadat of Makkah agreed on it. The key bearer of Ka'aba unlocked the Ka'aba. They entered the Ka'aba and observed the walls. They found them unbalanced and agreed to demolish eastern and western walls. They further decided if the Yamani wall was weak it should also be demolished. This suggestion was sent to the scholars of Makkah if engineers say that the Yamani wall is weak enough to fall down. Should they be relied? Scholars and ministers agreed to it. The Engineers demolished the walls. They had started this work on 20th Jamadiulawwal 1630A.D. (1040 Hijrah). Later on it was constructed. During the construction Shareef Abdullah came with lime and showered to on the walls seeking the reward from Allah Almighty. On 10th Shaban, the curtains were removed from the Ka'aba as the construction was finished. Ka'aba was cleaned. On 23rd Shaban, Meezab was installed. Ka'aba was covered by sheet of cloth on Friday in the Holy month of Ramadan. All this was done on the orders of Sultan Murad Khan bin Sultan Ahamd bin Sultan Muhammad Khan. May Allah reward him.

History of Renovations and Inscriptions in Ka'aba

The name of Sultan Murad Khan has been inscribed on a marble on the wall of Ka'aba along with the history of its construction. It contains the following words.

First Inscription

بِسْمِ اللهِ الرَّحْمٰنِ الرَّحِيْمِ

In the name of Allah, the most Gracious, the most Merciful.

Oh Allah! Accept this humble works of our's No doubt, You are the best hearer and best knower. Through this renovation of this Holy and majestic House of Allah, we are seeking closeness of Almighty Allah.

Allah is far from all faults and flaws. His splendour is too high. The servant of Holy Makkah and Madina, Attendant to pilgrims of Hajj by sea and land, Sultan Murad Khan bin Sultan Ahmed Khan bin Sultan Mohammad Khan. May Allah keep his kingship lasting forever and help his Kingdom.

These words were written in the last days of holy month of Ramadan. This work was completed in 1630 A.D. (1040 Hijrah).

Completion of Construction:

We have mentioned previously about the most authentic writings regarding the construction of Holy Ka'aba. Most of the historians have mentioned that Qasi bin Kalab constructed holy Ka'aba when he was appointed the custodian of holy Ka'aba. Whereas some historians have mentioned that Adam's Son Shees (blessings of Allah be upon them) built Ka'aba. It may be true or false. As far the replacement of roof and renovation of stones of Ka'aba are concerned, many caliphs and Kings have been doing those works. For example Waleed bin Abdul Malik, affixed marble tiles on floors of Ka'aba. Abu Jaffar Mansoor did some modifications in the walls of Baithullah. Taqi Fasi said I do not know whether the roof of Ka'aba was built or its ground and walls were constructed during the period of Abu Jaffar Mansoor.

Second Inscription

Inside the western wall of Holy Kaaba, the following composition is written on a marble slab.

بِسْمِ اللهِ الرَّحْمٰنِ الرَّحِيْمِ

In the name of Allah, the most Gracious, the most Merciful.

The decree for building the great House of Allah was conferred by the greatest Imam, Ameer ul Momineen, Abu Jaffer Mansoor Mustanser Billah. May Allah Almighty accept all his deeds.

This order was given on 1231 A.D. (629 Hijrah) May Almighty Allah bestow all His blessings and peace upon our commander Muhammad and his offspring.

This fact testifies that Abu Jaffer Mansoor also built some portions of Baithullah. Mutawakkul Abbasi changed the lower frame of door of Baithullah. It was made of a wood Sakho and was made silver plated. Muktafi Abbasi, made Meezab-e-Rehmat in 1146 (541 Hijrah) Nasir Abbasi, silver plated it in 1378 A.D. (780 Hijrah).

Third Inscription

King of Yaman Muzaffar, reconstructed Kaaba with stones and inscribed the following composition on marble on the interior western wall of Baithullah.

بِسْمِ اللّٰهِ الرَّحْمٰنِ الرَّحِيْمِ

In the name of Allah, the most Gracious, the most Merciful.

Oh! My Lord bestows me your guidance to offer to you my gratitude for your blessings on me and my father. Help us to perform righteous deeds for approval of your consent. Oh Merciful bestow your blessings on our chief Mohammad (peace and blessings of Allah upon Him) and his offspring's.

He ordered for renewal of marble of Baithullah. A needy servant of our Lord! favour and kindness Yosuf bin Umer bin Ali bin Rasool. Oh! Allah endorse me through Your predominant victory and O Merciful, O Forgiver, grant him pardon by virtue of your blessings.

This above inscription was written on 1282 A.D. (680 Hijrah). May Allah bestow His Salutation on our Lord Mohammad (peace and blessings of Allah upon Him), his offspring's and companions.

Fourth Inscription

Sultan Abu Nasr Burasbai uprooted the western stone of Baithullah and in its place on the other wall that is the interior wall of Ka'aba affixed a marble stone which contained the following composition.

O Allah grant acceptance for deed of our's. Without doubt You are best hearer best knower, majestic and dignified. Through renewed work of this tablet of House of Allah, the destitute servant of Allah, Sultan Malik Abu Nasr Burasbai, the servant of Holy Ka'aba and Prophet's Mosque, seeks the vicinity of Almighty Allah. May Allah grant him a good ending and make his deeds righteous. This composition has been written in 1423 A.D. (826 Hijrah).

It was renowned by Malik Moeed Sulan Qayatbai and after writing his name on this tablet then affixed it inside Holy Ka'aba. He inscribed the following phraseology on it.

بِسۡمِ اللهِ الرَّحۡمٰنِ الرَّحِيۡمِ

In the name of Allah, the most Gracious, the most Merciful.

O Allah grant acceptance for this work of our's. No doubt You are the best hearer. Sultan Malik Ashraf Qayatbai ordered for the renewal of inside tablet of Baithullah. O Lord of universes makes his Kingdom lasting forever. This writing was completed in the month of Rajab in 1479 A.D. (884 Hijrah).

Renewals in Ottoman Caliphate

The love and honor for the House of Allah by Ottoman Caliphate continued since centuries till todate. We have mentioned the works of Sutan Murad Khan earlier. Now we would mention about works of some more kings.

Fifth Inscription:

Sultan Suleman bin Sultan Saleem Khan repaired the two broken woods inside the Ka'aba. He repaired it in the presence of scholars. He made changes in the door, the sill of Ka'aba and Meezab of Rahmat.

Sixth Inscription:

Sultan Muhammad Khan renewed the roof of Ka'aba. He installed a tablet on the inside wall. The following words were inscribed on it:

بِسْمِ اللّٰهِ الرَّحْمٰنِ الرَّحِيْمِ

In the name of Allah, the most Gracious, the most Merciful.

O Allah please accept this work of ours. The order for the renewal of roof and interior and external portion of Holy Ka'aba was given by Sultan bin Sultan, Sultan Muhammad Khan in 1657 A.D. (1070 Hijrah). May Allah keep his Caliphate lasting for ever.

Seventh Inscription:

The late mother of Sultan Mustafa Khan had also the honor to contribute in the reconstruction work of Ka'aba. She discarded the additions made in the building. She installed a tablet on the wall. The writing is as follows:

بِسْمِ اللّٰهِ الرَّحْمٰنِ الرَّحِيْمِ

In the name of Allah, the most Gracious, the most Merciful.

The mother of Sultan Mustafa Khan did reconstruction work for House of Allah. May Allah always help her. She hopes through kindness of

Allah to pardon her sins. This work was completed in 1697 A.D. (1109

Hijrah). Alteration works in the building of Ka'aba were the regular

feature from time to time from the ancient period. The modification in

the roof, door and the Black Stone were carried out in different times.

The epoch of Sultan Abdul Hamid Khan bin Sultan Abdul Majid was

also featured with the changes. The last alterations took place in 1912

A.D. (1331 Hijrah) when the Black Stone was covered by a silver cage.

This was done in the era of Khadim Haramain Sharifain Ghazi

Muhammad Irshad Khan bin Sultan Mabroor Abdul Majeed Khan. [1]

---

[1] *The King of Yaman Tabaa went out to conquer the world. He had a gigantic army and four hundred very learned strong scholars accompanying him. He reached Makkah, but he was not honoured by the people of Makkah. He asked his companions why they did not pay respect to him which he deserved. They replied that they respect none but House of Allah. Suddenly the King fell the victim to an incurable and fatal illness. Inspite of best effort but Hakims he could not be healed up. Then one day, one of his ministers asked him in solitude about his intentions when he was not honoured by the people of Makkah. King said that he thought to destroy Kaaba to avenge his disgrace and punish the people. His minister told him that the fatal disease is a punishment from God so try to change your mind and try to please the people of Makkah. When the King repented and appealed to Allah for forgiveness, he soon recovered from the fatal disease. He arranged many feasts for the people of Makkah and covered the House of Allah with the first ever cover. It was made of silken cloth. This historic reference has been authenticated by a saying of our Holy Prophet (peace and blessings of Allah be upon him). He said*

"Don't scold Asad Haameri (King Tabaa) as he is the first one who provided a cover for House of Allah for the first time."

Covering of Ka'aba

Prophet Muhammad (peace and blessings of Allah be upon him) said on the day of the conquest of Makkah "Allah has honored the Ka'aba on this day. Ka'aba will be covered on the same day".[1]

The forthcoming traditions indicate that Ismaeel (blessing of Allah be upon him), Adnan and Tbaa covered the Ka'aba with the cover of Intaa.[2] and Wassail.[3] For the first time Ka'aba was coverd with Deebaj cloth by the following six persons.

1. Khalid
2. Nateela
3. Maawiya
4. Yazid
5. Ibn Zubair
6. Hajjaj

Ibn Hajr reports with reference to Wahab ibn Munabba that according to some people Prophet Muhammad (peace and blessings of Allah be upon him) had forbidden to abuse the tribe of Asad because they were the first to cover the holy building with Wasail.[4]

---

[1] Rawah-ul-Bukhari
[2] Clothe made in Yamen
[3] Colored leather based cloth
[4] Fath-ul-Bari

Abdur Razzaq reports that King Tabba was the first to cover the Holy
Ka'aba with Wassail. Some scholars thinks that Ismaeel (blessings of
Allah be upon him) was the first who covered Ka'aba. Zubair Ibn-e-
Bakaar reports that Adnan was the first who cover the Ka'aba and laid
the foundation of Ka'aba and Insaab (the stones that were erected
around Ka'aba for sacrificing animals). Balazari narrates a tradition that
Adnan bin Ado was the first one to cover the Ka'aba with Intaa. Waqidi
reports that the cloth was put on as cover on Ka'aba in the days of
ignorance. Than our Holy Prophet Muhammad (peace and blessings
of Allah be upon him) covered Ka'aba with a Yamani Cloth. Then Umar
(Allah be pleased with him) and Uthman Qibati covered Ka'aba. Thereafter
Hajjaj covered Ka'aba with Deebaj cloth. Imam Abi Sheebah narrated
that the covering of Ka'aba in the era of our Holy Prophet Muhammad
(peace and blessings of Allah be upon him) was made of Intaa.
Another tradition says that the elites of Arab covered the sacred building
with Qibati. Abdur Razzaq reports with his own reference that Aisha
(Allah be pleased with her) was inquired about the covering of Ka'aba.
She replied that the elites are enough to render this service. Another
tradition says that Deebaj was first covered by Abdullah bin Zubair (Allah
be pleased with him). Ibn Hajr says that the narrater of this tradition is
weak.Waqidi reports that Yazid bin Maawiya covered the Ka'aba with
Debaj. Ishaq bin Abi Farwa is weak narrater in this tradition.

Abdur Razzaq reports that Umar (Allah be pleased with him) used to cover the Ka'aba with Qibati [1]. Chain of transmitters have reported that Prophet Muhammad (peace and blessings of Allah be upon him), Abu Bakr, Umar and Uthman (Allah be pleased with them) covered the building of Ka'aba with Qibati and Hibrat. Deebaj was first covered by Abdul Malik bin Marrwan. All the jurists could not help appreciating it as the best cloth to match the dignity of Holy Ka'aba.

Fakehi reports that a carpet made of Deebaj was brought to Khalid bin Jaffer bin Kalad in the days of ignorance. That carpet was sent to the Ka'aba. Ka'aba was covered by it. According to Fakehi he was the first to cover the Ka'aba with Deebaj. Amadar Qutni narrates that Binte Deebaj was the first to cover the Ka'aba with Deebaj.

She was the mother of Abbas (Allah be pleased with him) bin Abdulmuttalib was lost somewhere in his childhood. She made a vow that if Abbas (Allah be pleased with him) comes back she would cover the Ka'aba with Deebaj. Zubair bin Bakaar says that when Zarrar bin Abdul Muttalib was lost his mother made a vow that if she gets him she would cover the Ka'aba.

---

[1] Qibati: A special type of linseed plant which is used for making cloth.

A man suffering from leprosy brought him to her. She covered the Ka'aba with white cloth.

All the above mentioned events show that the Ka'aba was covered with sheets of cloth many times on different occasions. Azraqi says that Maawiya (Allah be pleased with him) covered the Ka'aba with Deebaj[1], Qibati and Hibrat[2]. On each Ashoora (Tenth of Muharram-ul-Haram) Ka'aba was used to be covered by Deebaj. In the last days of the Holy month of Ramadan Ka'aba used to be covered by Qibat.

To sum up Ismaeel (blessing of Allah be upon him), Adnan, and Tabaa covered the Ka'aba with covering. One of the following was the first one who covered the Ka'aba with Deebaj.

1. Khalid   2.   Nateela   3.   Maawiya

4. Yazid   5.   Ibn Zubair   6.   Hajjaj

The tradition had already been quoted that Holy Prophet Muhammad (peace and blessings of Allah be upon him), Abu Bakr, Umar and Uthman (Allah be pleased with them) had covered the Ka'aba with different covers. A few traditions denied that in the eras of Abu Bakr and Umar (Allah be pleased with them) the Ka'aba was covered with sheaths.

---

[1] Deebaj: A beautiful cloth decorated with silk. The cover made of it was very excellent and liked very much.
[2] Hibrat: A special Yamani cloth on wich very delicate work is done.

Covering of Ka'aba
by Abasaid Caliphs and Kings

The Ka'aba used to be covered thrice a year by Abasaid caliphs. This was started particularly in the era of Mamoon bin Haroon Rasheed. He issued a decree that the Ka'aba should be covered thrice a year. Ka'aba used to be covered by Deebaj on the day of Arafa, Qibati on the first Rajab and white Deebaj on the first Shawwal.

Mutawakil increased the number of the covers in the month of Rajab. It used to be worn out because of the innumerable touches of the people's hands in this month. He also asked to hang the red Deebaj on the Ka'aba. This was done in 854A.D. (240 Hijrah). The removed covers of Ka'aba used to be kept by the servants of the House of Allah. The tradition from Aisha (Allah be pleased with her) indicates this fact.

Covering of Ka'aba by the Kings of Egypt and Yaman

The kings of Egypt and Yaman followed the Abasaids in covering the Ka'aba. Egyptian King Malik Salih bin Sultan bought the two villages, the earnings of which were fixed for the covering of Ka'aba.[1]

Egyptian Kings used to send the cover of Ka'aba. They used to send the external cover in black colour & the internal cover in red.

For the house of the Holy Prophet Muhammad (peace and blessings of Allah be upon him), they used to send green cover was is concerned they used to send green cover. On each cover the first Kalima was written. "There is no god but Allah Muhammad is His Prophet".

---

[1] The names of the villages were: Beeswis and Sandbees

Covering of Ka'aba by the Emperors of Ottoman Empire

When the family of Uthman Saleem Khan bin Sultan Bayazid Khan took over, they used to get prepared the internal and external covers of Ka'aba along with the cover for the house of Holy Prophet Muhammad (peace and blessings of Allah be upon him). The two villages that were appropriated for the purpose became too weak to generate the required funds to prepare the covers of Ka'aba. The king ordained to fill the remainder funds from Bait-ul-Mall. Some more areas were also specified for that purpose.

Sheikh Ali Tabri writes in his book, 'Tareekh-e-Makkah' that the external portion of the Ka'aba was covered with the black cover made of silk. The first Kalima was written on it. "There is no god but Allah, Muhammad is His Prophet".

On the day of sacrifice after Mina, Ramy, Jamrah and Aqbah, the Ka'aba used to be covered. Red cover was used for internal side of the Ka'aba. It had been a constant practice by the kings from the family of Ottoman. The removed covers were given to the family of Sheeba. They deserved it according to the Sharia and all scholare from Hanifi school of thought agreed to it. The kings of Egypt used to send the holy coverings of Ka'aba which were made up out of eight black sheets of silk. "There is no god but Allah, Muhammad is His

Prophet" was written in an arch shope on the cover. On both sides of cover "Jallajlalaho" and in the center 'Ya Allah' was written. One sheet was 15 meter long and about 15 meter wide. On every side of the Ka'aba from upto down, two sheets were hanged in such a way that they were encircled by brass. One can't realize that they are different sheets joined together and looked like a single sheet.

Writing on the Cover
of Ka'aba

There is a strap on the cover of Ka'aba with silver work on it. The

following verses are written in gilding on it.

بِسْمِ اللهِ الرَّحْمٰنِ الرَّحِيْمِ

وَاِذْ جَعَلْنَا الْبَيْتَ مَثَابَةً لِّلنَّاسِ وَاَمْنًا وَاتَّخِذُوْا مِنْ مَّقَامِ اِبْرٰهِمَ مُصَلًّى

وَعَهِدْنَآ اِلٰى اِبْرٰهِمَ وَاِسْمٰعِيْلَ اَنْ طَهِّرَا بَيْتِيَ لِلطَّآئِفِيْنَ وَالْعٰكِفِيْنَ وَالرُّكَّعِ

السُّجُوْدِ ۝ وَاِذْ قَالَ اِبْرٰهِمُ رَبِّ اجْعَلْ هٰذَا بَلَدًا اٰمِنًا وَّارْزُقْ اَهْلَهٗ مِنَ

الثَّمَرٰتِ مَنْ اٰمَنَ مِنْهُمْ بِاللهِ وَالْيَوْمِ الْاٰخِرِ قَالَ وَمَنْ كَفَرَ فَاُمَتِّعُهٗ قَلِيْلًا ثُمَّ

اَضْطَرُّهٗ اِلٰى عَذَابِ النَّارِ وَبِئْسَ الْمَصِيْرُ ۝ وَاِذْ يَرْفَعُ اِبْرٰهِمُ الْقَوَاعِدَ مِنَ

الْبَيْتِ وَاِسْمٰعِيْلُ رَبَّنَا تَقَبَّلْ مِنَّا اِنَّكَ اَنْتَ السَّمِيْعُ الْعَلِيْمُ ۝ رَبَّنَا وَاجْعَلْنَا

مُسْلِمَيْنِ لَكَ وَمِنْ ذُرِّيَّتِنَآ اُمَّةً مُّسْلِمَةً لَّكَ وَاَرِنَا مَنَاسِكَنَا وَتُبْ عَلَيْنَا

اِنَّكَ اَنْتَ التَّوَّابُ الرَّحِيْمُ ۝

And when We made the House (at Mecca) a resort for mankind and

a sanctuary, (saying): Take as your place of worship the place where

Abraham stood (to pray). And We imposed a duty upon Abraham and

Ishmael, (saying): Purify My house for those who go around and those

who meditate therein and those who bow down and prostrate

themselves (in worship).

And when Abraham prayed: My Lord! Make this a region of security and bestow upon its people fruits, such of them as believe in Allah and the Last Day, He answered: As for him who disbelieveth, I shall leave him in contentment for a while, then I shall compel him to the doom of fire--a hapless journey's end!

And when Abraham and Ishmael were raising the foundations of the House, (Abraham prayed): Our Lord! Accept from us (this duty). Lo! Thou, only Thou, art the Hearer, the Knower.

Our Lord! And make us submissive unto Thee and of our seed a nation submissive unto Thee, and show us our ways of worship, and relent toward us. Lo! Thou, only Thou, art the Relenting, the Merciful.[1]

On the Yamani side the following verse is written

بِسْمِ اللهِ الرَّحْمٰنِ الرَّحِيْمِ

﴿قُلْ صَدَقَ اللهُ فَاتَّبِعُوْا مِلَّةَ اِبْرٰهِيْمَ حَنِيْفًا وَمَا كَانَ مِنَ الْمُشْرِكِيْنَ ○
اِنَّ اَوَّلَ بَيْتٍ وُّضِعَ لِلنَّاسِ لَلَّذِىْ بِبَكَّةَ مُبٰرَكًا وَّهُدًى لِّلْعٰلَمِيْنَ ○ فِيْهِ
اٰيٰتٌ بَيِّنٰتٌ مَّقَامُ اِبْرٰهِيْمَ ○﴾

---

[1] Al Baqara : 125,126,127,128

Say: Allah speaketh truth. So follow the religion of Abraham, the upright. He was not of the idolaters.

Lo! the first Sanctuary appointed for mankind was that at Mecca, a blessed place, a guidance to the peoples;

Wherein are plain memorials (of Allah's guidance); the place where Abraham stood up to pray; and whosoever entereth it is safe. And pilgrimage to the House is a duty unto Allah for mankind, for him who can find a way thither. As for him who disbelieveth, (let him know that) Lo! Allah is Independent of (all) creatures.[1]

بِسْمِ اللهِ الرَّحْمٰنِ الرَّحِيْمِ

﴿ وَإِذْ بَوَّأْنَا لِإِبْرَاهِيْمَ مَكَانَ الْبَيْتِ اَنْ لَّا تُشْرِكْ بِيْ شَيْئًا وَّطَهِّرْ
بَيْتِيَ لِلطَّائِفِيْنَ وَالْقَائِمِيْنَ وَالرُّكَّعِ السُّجُوْدِ ۝ ﴾

And (remember) when We prepared for Abraham the place of the (Holy) House, saying: Ascribe thou no thing as partner unto Me, and purify My House for those who make the round (thereof) and those who stand and those who bow and make prostration.

---

[1] Al Imran : 95, 96, 97

And proclaim unto mankind the Pilgrimage. They will come unto thee on foot and on every lean camel; they will come from every deep ravine.[1]

On the western side the following verse is written.

بِسْمِ اللّٰهِ الرَّحْمٰنِ الرَّحِيمِ

﴿لِّيَشْهَدُوا مَنَافِعَ لَهُمْ وَيَذْكُرُوا اسْمَ اللّٰهِ فِىٓ اَيَّامٍ مَّعْلُوْمٰتٍ عَلٰى مَا رَزَقَهُمْ مِّنْ بَهِيْمَةِ الْاَنْعَامِ فَكُلُوْا مِنْهَا وَاَطْعِمُوا الْبَآئِسَ الْفَقِيْرَ ۞ ثُمَّ لِيَقْضُوْا تَفَثَهُمْ وَلْيُوْفُوْا نُذُوْرَهُمْ وَلْيَطَّوَّفُوْا بِالْبَيْتِ الْعَتِيْقِ ۞﴾

That they may witness things that are of benefit to them, and mention the name of Allah on appointed days over the beast of cattle that He hath bestowed upon them. Then eat thereof and feed therewith the poor unfortunate.

Then let them make an end of their unkemptness and pay their vows and go around the ancient House.[2]

On the eastern side of Meezab the following writing is found:

---

[1] Al Hajj : 26, 27
[2] Al Hajj : 27, 28

The Ruling for the use of the covers of Ka'aba

As per opinions of so many scholars it is permissible to use the Cast-off covers of Ka'aba. They argue from the traditions of their ancestor scholars. Aisha (Allah be pleased with her) had given fatwa to sell and use of it. She further said that an impure (junbi) can wear something made out of it.

Ibn Hajr reports with refernce to Fakihi's Akhbar Makia Aisha (Allah be pleased with her) says that once Ali Sheeba came to me and said that he had many covers of the Ka'aba. He inquired if he should bury them so that impure can not wear it. She replied that he was wrong. He could sell them. The money can be spent on indigents. If impure wears them that was not bad.[1]

Sheeba used to send them to Yaman to sell. He used to spend the money where Aisha (Allah be pleased with her) ordered him. Ibn Abtal says that the rational behind it, is that the servants of Ka'aba could be benefited.

Zuhri and Fakehi narrate that the sunnah and the verdict of Aisha (Allah be pleased with her) show that the cover was to be given to the

---
[1] Fath-ul-Bari

Sheikh in the era of Prophet. Sheeba was not aware of its use. That
was the reason he inquired Aisha (Allah be pleased with her) about
it. She verdicted to sell, use and even an impure can wear it. After
coming to know the right use of cover, Sheeba started using it. Once
the thing is used and it can be lost if kept longer. Hence it is better to
sell it and use its money. The servants of Ka'aba deserve more than
any body else to use it.

Tabri writes in "Tareekh-e- Makkah" (History of Makkah) that whenever
either of the sheets was removed the family of Sheeba deserved more.
A good number of Hanifi scholars verdicted on its permissibility.

Qutb-ud-din Hanify writes that if Waqif does not put away any condition,
the practice would be to follow the past. The cover of Ka'aba is
managed through the Auqaf. The Auqaf 's condition is not known. It
is the habit of the family of Sheeba that they take the cast-off covers
of Ka'aba. They would continue to follow this tradition. This is the
argument to use the cover of Ka'aba and to use the money after selling
it. A good number of people show their eagerness to purchase
purchase the covers of Ka'aba.

Gifts and Hanging Objects in Ka'aba

People from the unknown time have been presenting a lot of gifts to the Ka'aba. Abdullah bin Zubair (Allah be pleased with him) got the pillars of Ka'aba made of gold. Abdul Malik bin Marwan gave 30,000 deenar of gold so as to get the door, pillars and the interior of Ka'aba decorated. He did that. So far the treasure of Ka'aba is concerned, the servants of Ka'aba used to take it as previously practiced. It was also the commandment of the caliph. Muhammad bin Haroon-ur-Rashid gave Salim bin Jarrah 18000 deenar. He got the door and its sill decorated with gold. The rest of the gifts of Ka'aba were taken by the servants of Ka'aba. It is said that Mutawakil Abbasi got repaired one side of the Ka'aba by gold and decorated both sides of the door with gold.The mother of Muqtader Abbasi also decorated the pillars of Ka'aba. Muqtafi made a new door of Ka'aba with gold. He gave the previous door to the servants of Ka'aba. He got made his coffin out of the wood taken from Ka'aba, so that he should be buried in it. I would particularly mention the Egyptian kings Malik Nasir Qalawoon and Sultan Sulman Khan. He set new patterns in the decoration of Ka'aba. Similarly Sultan Murad Khan renewed the building of Mosque of Al Haram. May Allah be pleased with him.

Fasi says that when Malik Nasir Qalawoon performed Hajj he ordered to replace the old door with new one. The family of Sheeba took the old door. Fasi says that it has been proved from Holy Prophet Muhammad (peace and blessings of Allah be upon him), righteous caliphs and kings that the family of Sheeba deserves the removed objects of the Ka'aba. None would share that according to the ruling of Sharia.

Summary

The gifts and other offerings presented to Ka'aba is the right of the family of Sheeba. None deserves them other than the family of Sheeba. If it were not, Umar (Allah be pleased with him) would have used them. As the tradition reflects that he wanted to distribute among the poor. Sheeba told him that it was against the practice of Holy Prophet (peace and blessing of Allah be upon him) and Abu Bakr (Allah be pleased with him). When they did not use it how others could use them without the prior permission of the family of Sheeba.

Theft of the objects of Ka'aba

Many thieves managed to steal things from Ka'aba. The most shameful event took place in the era of Muqtadar Abbasi. The group of Qaramit used to loot the caravans heading to perform Hajj so that they should do the Hajj of Hajr. It was a town of Bahrain. This was led by Abu Tahir Qaramti. Abu Tahir entered the mosque of Al Haram and martyred 30000 people offering Hajj. He looted the gold and silver of Ka'aba. He uprooted the door of Ka'aba and threw the dome of Zamzam. He went back to his own town.

Entering Ka'aba
and offering prayer:

The Sahih traditions reflect that the Prophet and his righteous companions entered the Ka'aba. Hence it is sunnah. Bukhari divided all the relevant Ahadith into the following four chapters.

1.   For those who closed the door of Ka'aba and offered prayer.

2.   For those who offer prayer in the Ka'aba

3.   For those Who did not enter Ka'aba

4.   For those Who said Takbeer in any corner of Ka'aba

Bukhari relies on the tradition from Abdullah bin Umar (Allah be pleased with him). He said that Holy Prophet along with Usama bin Zaid, Bilal, Uthman bin Talha entered Ka'aba and shut its door. When they opened it and entered first and asked Bilal if Prophet offered prayer in the Ka'aba. He replied "yes" he had offered prayer in between these two Yamani pillars.

Ibn Hajr writes that Holy Prophet offered in between the two front pillars.[1] He records from the Malik Nafie that there was one pillar on the right side of Prophet and there was another on his left. Another tradition says that there were six pillars of Ka'aba and Prophet Muhammad (peace and blessings of Allah be upon him) offered prayers in between the first two pillars.

---

[1] Fath-ul-Bari

The door of Ka'aba was on the back of Prophet Muhammad (peace and blessings of Allah be upon him). Yet another tradition says that where Prophet offered prayer there was red stone. All these traditions are after the Ka'aba was reconstructed by Abdullah bin Zubair (Allah be pleased with him). Nafie records that where Prophet stood to offer prayer there was a distance of three yards between the Prophet and the wall of Ka'aba. Abu Daud reports that where Prophet offered prayer there was a distance of 3 yards between the Qibla and the Prophet himself. Ibne Hajr says whoever wants to follow the Prophet in this regard he should keep the distance of 3 yards from the wall of Ka'aba. Following that way would lead the situation to such that man would touch the same ground where Prophet did. In the second chapter, Ibn Umar reports that whenever he enters the Ka'aba in the straight direction, the door of Ka'aba would be at the back of him. Until there remain 3 yards distance between him and the wall. He offered prayer trying to offer at the same place where Prophet did according to the narration of Bilal (Allah be pleased with him) However man can offer the prayer wherever he likes. In the third chapter, Bukhari relies on the tradition from Abdullah bin Ubai Aofi that Holy Prophet had offered the Umra, circumambulated the Ka'aba and offered two cycles of ritual services behind the place of Ibrahim (blessings of Allah be upon him). He was surrounded by the people. One asked if Prophet entered the Ka'aba.

The narrator said no. Nawavi reports recorded by Ibn Hajr that Prophet Muhammad (peace and blessings of Allah be upon him) did not enter Ka'aba because of the presence of idols and fresco paintings. Pagans did not permit Prophet to remove them. On the conquest of Makkah he ordered to remove the paintings. When he entered the Ka'aba, it was free from idols. Similar tradition is reported from Ibne Abbas. In the fourth chapter Bukhari relies on the report from Ibne Abbas that when Prophet came in Makkah. He declined to enter the Ka'aba, as the idols were kept there. Prophet ordered to remove them. He also ordered to remove the pictures of Ibrahim and Ismaeel (blessings of Allah be upon them). Then entered the Ka'aba and pronounced takbeer and did not offer prayer. I say that the tradition of Ibn Abbas goes against the tradition of Ibn Umar in which he asked Bilal (Allah be pleased with him) if Prophet offered prayer. He said yes. Ibn Hajr says that in the tradition of Ibne Abbas Prophet pronounced Takbeer but did not offer prayer. Where as Bilal did not reject that he did not pronounce Takbeer.

The tradition of Bilal (Allah be pleased with him) reflects that Prophet offered the prayer whereas tradition of Ibne Abbas negates that. The author abstracts that on that day Prophet was not accompanied by Ibne Abbas. Prophet's prayer in the Ka'aba was negated by Usama and Fazal. Both of them are not proved to be with the Prophet on that day. Hence negation is controversial whereas affirmation is clear.

The tradition of Bilal (Allah be pleased with him) would be preferred Nawavi and a chain of transmitters say that the affirmation of Bilal and the negation of Usama can be reconciled when he entered along with Prophet. He might have seen Prophet praying. Following him he would also offer prayer. For that purpose he stood in the corner of the Ka'aba. The door was shut and the room was dark. Prophet might have offered prayer and could not see him. Bilal (Allah be pleased with him) had seen Prophet because he was close to him. When Usama came out he denied that Prophet offered prayer.

The ruling for prayer in Ka'aba

This has been proved that Prophet offered prayer inside the Ka'aba. It has been recorded by Bukhari, Muslim and many others. Hence it is Sunnah.. The prayer of Tahiya ul Masjid is outside the Ka'aba. When Prophet came to Makkah, he offered prayer close to the Ka'aba.

This prayer might be seen as tahiya ul Masjid or it shows that Ka'aba is also a mosque. Allah knows best. So far congregational prayer is concerned inside Ka'aba, Imam Malik is against it. Congregational prayer is forbidden inside the Ka'aba. A few scholars are of the view that if it is deliberate he would pronounce it again. Others say he would offer it again in every situation deliberate or unknowingly.

Imam Tirmizi records from Imam Malik it is Nafl. Ibn Daqeeq al Eed says that Imam Malik forbids offering congregational prayer inside the Ka'aba. Similarly it is debateable to offer prayer in Hateem. We said so far to enter Ka'aba is good. To offer prayer in it is the Sunnah of Prophet . Bihiqi and ibn Khuzaima rely on the tradition of Ibn Abbas saying whoever entered the Ka'aba he entered with good and came out without any sin. Baihiqi says that Abdul Malik bin Momil is a weak narrator. Qartabi says that entering Ka'aba is a part of Hajj rites. It has been recorded in Fath ul Bari [1].

---

[1] *Hafiz bin Hijar Asqalani quoted in Fath ul Bari that prayer can be offered in every direction inside Baithullah. If Imam forms an assembly for prayers inside Baithullah and back of a follower comes towards Imam, the prayer will be done. But back of the follower should not be infront of the face of the Imam.*

A soothsayer said to Amr bin Amir that I intuited that the rock of Ahl
Marib has been broken. Flood may destroy the two gardens. Amr saw
a rat digging the rock. That rock blocked the water of flood. He
understood that rock would not remain for long. They came out of their
locality and destroyed everything that came in their way. They dragged
the natives out of their area. The soothsayer said that whatever I tell
you it is on behlaf of lord of Arabs and non Arabs.

They asked what to do. She asked to sacrifice a camel so that they
could live around the honorable place of Al Haram. When they reached
Makkah, they saw Jarham was their leader of them who had deprived
the descendents of Ismaeel (blessing of Allah be upon him). Salaba
bin Amr bin Aamir said we left our place. Everywhever we went the
people accommodated us. So that we could take rest here. We could
send our spies to Syria and East. We can adjust with you easily.
Jarham refused to accommodate them and asked them to leave that
area. Salaba responded him that they could not leave at least for one
year until their spies come back. If you adjust us happily we would
praise you. If not then we would fight against you and kill your males
and make your women as captives. Jarham declined.Hence there was
a furious war which lasted three days. Jarham was defeated in the
war. Midhad did not participate in the war and took his family away
and went to Qunoon and Hilli. Saalaba remained for one year in
Makkah. He got fever. He came to soothsayer. Tarifa said it is better
that we disintegrate.

They asked how. Whoever is grieved should go to Amman. They became Azd Amman later on. Those who are brave should go to Arak. They became are Khuzaa. Whoever want abundant food should go Yasrab. Dates are in abundance over there. Whoever wants kingdom should go to Basra and Aweer in Syria. They became the family of Jaffa. Whoever wants horses and treasury should go to Iraq. They became the family of Juzaima. When their spies came back they were divided into two groups. One group left for Amman. Saalaba went to Syria. Khuzaa are the descendents of those who settled in Makkah. Rabia bin Haritha bin Amr bin Amir became the custodian of Ka'aba. When this custodianship came to the Khuzaa, the descendants of Ismaeel (blessing of Allah be upon him) came to them. They sought permission to live there. Khuzaa did not allow them. When Midhad bin Amr sought the permission he was too refused because they did not support them in their war against their enemy. Rabia bin Haritha asked his nation to kill Jarhami wherever they find them. It is said that camel of Midhad fled to Makkah. He followed the footsteps and reached Makkah. He mounted on the mount of Abu Qubais. He saw that his camel was being slaughtered. He returned fearing that he might be slaughtered.

Key Bearers of Ka'aba in the times of Ignorance.

The descendents of Ismaeel (blessings of Allah be upon him) have long been honored with services of Ka'aba. This was taken by the tribe Jarham.Later Jarham were overthrown by the tribe Khuzaa. Qusai bin Kilab bin Murah managed to get that honor in their family. After him this was transferred in the tribe of his son Abd ud Dar. I shall briefly mention all of them.

Jarham

Muhay Uddin ibne Arabi writes in his book 'Muhadharat-ul-Abrar' that when it was prolonged Jarham started to be linient about the sanctity of the mosque Al Haram. They continued with this unbalanced treatment. If somebody would point out the mistakes, they would become harsh against him. Until they became disintegrated and started fighting against each other. They were considered nobles among the Arabs in their number of people and weapons. One man from their nation, Midhaad bin Amr, stood up to advise them. 'O people fear Allah and protect the sanctity of His House. The nations of Hood, Salih and Shoaib have been killed. Don't follow them. Invite people to good and forbid them from bad. Don't be lenient in keeping the chastity of the Al Haram. Now peace should not deceive you. He frightened them from Allah. They could not come back to peace. instead of it their insurgency heightened to a great extent. Then Midhaad buried the gold the two statues of deer at Zam Zam.

This work is done by the king of Arabs and non Arabs, the king of kings, Sultan Muhammad Rishad Khan V son of Sultan Abdul Majeed Khan son of Sultan Mehmood Khan Ghazi son of Sultan Abdul Hamid Khan son of Sultan Ahmad Khan son of Sultan Muhammad Khan son of Sultan Ibrahim Khan son of Sultan Murad Khan.

Be it known that whoever became king from the family of Uthman his name would have been remained written on the strap of cover of Ka'aba during his tenure. There are two sheets hanged on the walls of Ka'aba. One of them is hanged on the door and another inside the building. The third one is hanged on the Maqam-e-Ibrahim. It is decorated in the same way as the Hazam and the door of Ka'aba. It is engraved. The cost of the cover of Ka'aba, come to about 4555 Egyption Jineeh. The extracts of roses have also been sent by Egypt for cleaning of Ka'aba.

Qusai bin Kalab as custodian of Makkah

The custodianship came to the grand father of Prophet Muhammad (peace and blessings of Allah be upon him) after it. Quraish were responsible for the following services.

1.   Service of Ka'aba
2.   Dar-un-Nadwa
3.   Flag
4.   Hosting of pilgrims
5.   Watering service for pilgrims

Qusai used to do all these works himself. He had two sons. Elder was Abdud Dar and the younger was Manaf. Both of them were noble at the time of their father. When Qusai grew older he divided the work among these two brothers. Abdud Dar was given DarunNadwa, flag and the key. [1]

Abd Manaf [2] Abd Manaf 's name was Mugheera. He was handsome. People would call him Qamar-ul-Batha the moon of Batha. He had four sons. Hashim, Muttalib, Abd Shams, Nofil. Prophet was from the descendents of Hashim who was given the Siqayat (watering). Opening and closing the door was his responsibility. When Qusai passed away hosting pilgrims and Siqayat came in his share. Abdud Dar got the Hijabat, liwa, Darun Nadwa. This custodianship remained in the family of Abdud Dar. His son Usman bin Abdud Dar followed him. When

Quraish needed to counsil on any issue they used to open the Darun
Nadwa. Sadanat remained in the descendents of Abdud Dar Usman
bin Talha bin Abu Talha bin Abdul Uza bin Usman bin Abdud Dar bin
Qusai.

---

[1] *Hijaba was considerd the noblest designation. It refers the services of Ka'aba. Whoever
was given this honor was given the keys of Ka'aba. Opening and closing the doors
of Ka'aba were their responsibility. The goods were kept with Ka'aba.
It is their responsability to preserve them is the responsibility of them. Qusai encouraged
the people to be hospitable to the pilgrims. He raised funds to arrange feasts for the
pilgrims. It was called Rifadah. Siqaya was the service of watering pilgrims. Quraish
used to collect the water to give to the pilgrims. Darun Nadwa was a big building. Its
door opened in Al Haram. Quraish used to debate the forthcoming social, political
and economic problems. It was a sort of Parliament. Liwa means flag. It was like
defense ministry. If there was a collective danger he would hoist the flag in the open
ground. It was the signal to defend the city.*

Key Bearing of Ka'aba in Islam

Uthman-bin-Talha (Allah be pleased with him)

It is controversial when did he accept Islam. Was that after the conquest of Makkah or before that? Most authentic traditions show that he accepted Islam before the conquest of Makkah. The traditions show that he accepted Islam on the day of the conquest of Makkah. Qastalani records in his Mawahib Luduunia with reference to Tabqat ibn Saad. Uthman says that we used to open the Ka'aba on Monday and Thursday in the days of ignorance. Once Prophet came to me wishing to go inside the Ka'aba along with other people. I reacted harshly (Allah forbid). Prophet replied "O Uthman you would soon see this key in my hands. Whomever I shal give it would become his". He said "on that day Quraish would be perished". Prophet said "no on that day they would be honored and respected". When Prophet entered the Ka'aba he recalled everything and thought all he said would happen. Prophet asked me to bring him the key. I obeyed He took it from me and gave it to me again. He said "the custodianship would remain in your family forever. None would take it away from you except a transgressor. O Uthman Allah made you responsible for this house. Take from it in an appropriate way. When Prophet returned me the key he said Is it not as I said.? I recalled that day when he said that one day this would be in his hands and to whom He gives, it would be his.

Interpretation of the Verse 58 of An Nisa

Allah says in the holy Quran

﴿ اِنَّ اللّٰهَ يَاْمُرُكُمْ اَنْ تُؤَدُّوا الْاَمٰنٰتِ اِلٰٓى اَهْلِهَا ﴾

Lo! Allah commandeth you that ye restore deposits to their owners.[1]

This verse was revealed on the day of the conquest of Makkah. Prophet entered the city as victorious. Uthman was the key bearer of Ka'aba. He locked the Ka'aba and mounted on the roof of it. Prophet wanted to remove the idols. For that he asked Ali (Allah be pleased with him) to bring the key. Ali (Allah be pleased with him) inquired about Uthman. People told him about Uthman. He asked for the key. Uthman declined. Ali managed to snatch the key and said " O Othman all people of Makkah depend on Prophet today". He presented the key to the Prophet. He freed the Ka'aba from Idols and offered two cycles of prayer. When Prophet came out of Ka'aba Abbas (Allah be pleased with him) asked Prophet that Siqayat is my responsibility so assign the responsability of key bearing to me as well. On this occasion this verse was revealed. Restore deposits to their owners. Prophet asked He to return the key to Uthman. Ali (Allah be pleased with him) went to Uthman and returned him the key of Ka'aba. Uthman said why did you return it to me. He said that this verse is revealed. Uthman was impressed by it and accepted Islam.

---

[1] Al-Nisa : 58

Gibreel (blessings of Allah be upon him) came and said as long as Ka'aba remains, the family of Uthman would be the key bearers of this house. He gave the key to his nephew Sheeba before he died. From that day on the family of Sheeba continued to be the custodian of Ka'aba and will remain till the day of judgement.[1]

Kalbi records that when Prophet asked for the key. Uthman extended his hand to give it to the Prophet. Abbas (Allah be pleased with him) asked Prophet if he should add key responsibility with Siqaya. Uthman withdrew his hand. Prophet asked him if he believed in Allah and the day of Judement. Give him the key. He gave it to the Prophet. The verse revealed then. Ibne Zafar says this tradition is authentic.

All the traditions from ibne Saad negate that Uthman accepted Islam before the conquest of Makkah. Since Prophet reminded him ...... so uthman said I attest that you Muhammad (peace and blessing of Allah be upon him) is His Prophet. This shows that he was Muslim and this attestation was repetition. If somebody attests late he then becomes Muslim. It is also possible that he withdrew and again became Muslim. A tradition from Bukhari indicates this. Many other traditions also indicate the same theme recorded by Hafiz ibn AbdulBar, ibn Hajr and Ibn Katheer. Ibn Kateer writes that this verse was particularly revealed in the favour of Uthman bin Talha bin Abi Talha. Abu talha was from the descendents of Qusai bin Kilab. He was the Hajib of Ka'aba. He was the nephew of sheeba bin uthman bin Abu Talha. The key

---

[1] Tabri, Rooh-ul-Maani, Tafseer Kabeer

remained in their family till today. They accepted Islam during truce of Hudaibia and conquest of Makkah. When Khalid bin Walid and Amr bin Aas accepted Islam. His uncle fought against Muslims in the battle of Uhad and was killed in that state. (non Muslim)

We have described the genealogy because a lot of interpreters have been doubtful about it.

Muhammad bin Ishaq writes that people were content when Prophet came to Makkah. He took seven circumambulations of the Ka'aba. After accomplishing it he asked Uthman for the key. He took the key and entered the House of Allah. He broke the sculpture of a bird. He stood at the door of Ka'aba. People gathered in the compound. Ibne Ishaq says that Prophet said " All praises belong to Allah. He made his promise true. He helped His men and defeated the enemy. Every thing of the day of ignorance is under my feet except watering the pilgrims and the key of Ka'aba. He sat in the mosque. Ali (Allah be pleased with him) asked the Prophet holding the key of Ka'aba that if we should perform both the responsibilities. Prophet called Uthman. He gave Uthman the key and said it is a day of virtue and loyalty.[1]

Ibn Jareer says that this verse was revealed about Uthman bin Talha.

When Prophet took the key from Uthman and entered the Ka'aba on the day of the Conquest of Makkah. He came out of Ka'aba reciting this verse.

---

[1] Seerathu-un-Nabi : vol : 4, p :31, 32

$$\text{﴿ اِنَّ اللّٰهَ يَأْمُرُكُمْ اَنْ تُؤَدُّوا الْاَمٰنٰتِ اِلٰٓى اَهْلِهَا ﴾}$$

Lo! Allah commandeth you that ye restore deposits to their owners,[1]
He called Uthman and handed over the key of Ka'aba. Umar bin
Khattab (Allah be pleased with him) said when Prophet came out he
was reciting this verse Lo! Allah commandeth you that ye restore
deposits to their owners,[2] I did not listen Prophet reciting this verse
ever before.

Ibne Abbas (Allah be pleased with him) narrates about this verse
Lo! Allah commandeth you that ye restore deposits to their owners,[3]
When Prophet conquered the Makkah he called Uthman to show him
the key. When he gave the key, Abbas requested the Prophet if we
could take this responsibility along with watering. Listening that, Uthman
withdrew his hand. Prophet again asked Uthman for the key. He again
extended his hand. Abbas (Allah be pleased with him) repeated the
same. Uthman withdrew again. Prophet said if you believe on the
Day of Judgment and Allah give this key to me.

He opened the door and saw the pictures of Ibrahim (blessings of
Allah be upon him). He removed the pictures and brought the place
of Ibrahim (blessings of Allah be upon him) out of Ka'aba and said

---

[1] Al Nisa
[2] Al Nisa
[3] Al Nisa

that this is Qibla. He circumambulated twice. Gabriel (blessings of Allah be upon him) came and asked Prophet to return the key. Prophet recited the verse

$$﴿ اِنَّ اللّٰهَ يَأْمُرُكُمْ اَنْ تُؤَدُّوا الْاَمٰنٰتِ اِلٰٓى اَهْلِهَا ٥٨ ﴾$$

Lo! Allah commandeth you that ye restore deposits to their owners.[1]

The opinions of Jurists on the Key Bearing

Ibn Ishaq writes in Seerat ibn Hisham that Khuzaa continued to serve Ka'aba till Halil bin Habisha. He was the last custodian.[2]

---

[1] Al-Nisa: 58
[2] Seerat Ibne Hisham

The saying of Holy Prophet (peace and blessings of Allah be upon him) about Key Bearing

Muhammad Yahya Khitab Maliki says when the people disagree on the habit and tradition, the elder's Urf can be the basis of decision. Since habit is decisive in many matters.

Ibne Zahiria writes that when the people of Ka'aba disagree on any issue. The decision is made on the basis of elderhood. Holy Prophet (peace and blessings of Allah be upon him) said that this key is not given by me, it is given by Allah. Prophet further said that every family's respect is under my feet except the key and water services. In another tradition he says that respect the House of Allah. and the key bearers.

The verdicts of Scholors about Services, Covers & Gifts

A question was raised before the Mufti of Makkah Syed Abdullah bin Muhammadul Mir Hanifi about the ruling of services, gifts ,internal and external covers of Ka'aba and vows. Is it legitimate for Bani sheeba to get them? Can anybody else share it? He answered "all is related to the family of Sheeba". It will remain with them till the day of Judgment This is supported by the verses of holy Quran, the traditions of the Prophet; verdicts of the scholars. It is not permissible for a man to be ambiguous about it if he believes in Allah and the Day of Judgment. If somebody commits that he would be cursed by Allah, if he is going against the traditions of the Prophet. It is the duty of the Ameer to be strict in this matter to keep the people according to the saying of the Prophet. Follow the footsteps of the Prophet Muhammad (peace and blessings of Allah be upon him) and be among the people who are liked by Allah. As Allah says in the holy Quran:

﴿ قُلْ اِنْ كُنْتُمْ تُحِبُّوْنَ اللّٰهَ فَاتَّبِعُوْنِيْ يُحْبِبْكُمُ اللّٰهُ وَ يَغْفِرْلَكُمْ ذُنُوْبَكُمْ ط وَاللّٰهُ غَفُوْرٌ رَّحِيْمٌ ۝ ﴾

Say, (O Muhammad, to mankind): If ye love Allah, follow me; Allah will

love you and forgive you your sins. Allah is Forgiving, Merciful.[1]

Allama Abu Saood writes in his Tafseer that Lo! Allah commandeth

you that ye restore deposits to their owners. This verse was revealed

about Uthman bin Abu Talha who was the key bearer of Ka'aba. He

narrated the complete tradition.

The same question was answered by Mufti Sheikh Jamal Hanafi that

serving Ka'aba ,closing and opening its door is the sole responsibility

of the family of Sheeba. He is the descendent of Uthman bin Talha.

All the traditions of the Prophet indicate that this remained in his family

in the days of ignorance as well as in the days of Islam. On the

Conquest of Makkah Holy Prophet took key from Uthman. He was

thinking that holy Prophet would not return him the key. Abbas bin

Abdul Muttalib (Allah be pleased with him) requested the Prophet to

give him this responsibility as well. Allah revealed this verse Lo! Allah

commandeth you that ye restore deposits to their owners. Umar bin

Khattab (May Allah be pleased with him) said when Prophet was

reciting this verse. I did not listen Prophet reciting this verse ever

before. He called the Uthman and handed over the key. He said you

will keep it forever.

Fakehi Jabeer bin Mutaam reports that when Prophet handed the

---

[1] Al-e-Imran : 31

Key over to Uthman, he asked him to hide it. All the above mentioned
traditions reveal this fact that this responsibility was given to the family
of Sheeba by Prophet and Allah. This responsibility remained assigned
to them in the days of ignorance as well as in the days of Islam. Ameer
following the footsteps of Prophet should not see their errors. The
family may use the gifts and foodstuff presented to Ka'aba in a decent
manner as the tradition of the Prophet prevails. Hence it is permissible
for them.

Fasi records an event when Nasir Muhammad bin Qlawoon performed
Hajj. he replaced the door of Ka'aba with new one. The removed door
was taken by the people of Ka'aba. Fasi remarked that whenever
there comes any change in the Ka'aba, older or cost-of stuff would
belong to the people of Ka'aba(the family of Sheeba). It is their old
custom.

Syed Abdullah Muraghani, Mufti of Makkah, says "anybody believes
in the day of Judgement and Allah should not be dubious in it and nor
hurt the Sheeba. He would be cursed otherwise.

Sheikh Abdullah Siraj Hanifi says that the family of Sheeba is the key
bearer from the time of Prophet till the Day of Judgment. As many
traditions of the Prophet reflect this fact. None would ever share in
these services with them. Allah almighty says

﴿ اِنَّ اللّٰهَ يَاْمُرُكُمْ اَنْ تُؤَدُّوا الْاَمٰنٰتِ اِلٰٓى اَهْلِهَا ٥ ﴾

Lo! Allah commandeth you that ye restore deposits to their owners.

Imam Ahmad says that this verse was revealed about the key bearer

of Ka'aba Uthman bin Abi Talha. Zubair bin Mutama says that Gabriel

(blessings of Allah be upon him) said to Prophet that till the Day of

Judgment, the family of Sheeba will remain responsible for the House

of Allah.

Bisher bin sara writes in "Al Manasik" that Abu Hanifa entered the

Ka'aba, offered the prayer and gave 1000 deenar to the family of

Sheeba. He said that they are the legitimate key bearers of the House

of Allah. Imam Malik says that none is going to share the treasury of

Ka'aba with them because it has been given to Uthman by Holy Prophet

Muhammad (peace and blessing of Allah be upon him). Qazi Ayyaz

says that the treasury is the property of the House of Allah. The family

of Sheeba can use them in an appropriate way. This is permissible

to them. Similarly the old cover of Ka'aba is also their property. They

can use as they wish. If they stop somebody to enter the Ka'aba he

can't enter. Aisha (Allah be pleased with her) asked Prophet why the

door of Ka'aba was so high. Prophet replied that it is because your

nation could stop anybody.

Another tradition tells Aisha (May Allah be pleased with her) said

"every wife of Prophet entered the Ka'aba except her. Prophet asked

her to seek permission from Sheeba. You can be permitted because

you have close family terms with them. She contacted them. They came to Prophet saying that the door of Ka'aba is not opened at night both in the days of ignorance and in the days of Islam. If you say we can open that. Prophet took Aisha (Allah be pleased with her) with her hand and asked her to offer her prayers in Hateem.[1]

To hide the key of Ka'aba is permissible. Jubair bin Mutama records that Prophet gave the key to Uthmman and asked him to hide it. Zahri says that key is hided because he can not be terminated unless he himself resigns. This is the saying of Allah and his Prophet. (Abdullah bin Abdurahman Siraj).

Abdurahman Siraj, the son of Abdullah Siraj said that whatever my father, my teacher Jamal bin Abdullah Hanafi and Syed Abdullah Murghani said is correct and I support it . Allah knows the best. Sheikh Abbas bin Siddique Hanafi replies to the question. The family of Sheeba is the custodian of the Ka'aba till the Day of Judgment. Lo! Allah commandeth you that ye restore deposits to their owners. Holy Prophet took the key from Uthman the nephew of Sheeba bin Talha and entered the Ka'aba. The verse reveals

$$\text{﴿ اِنَّ اللّٰهَ يَأْمُرُكُمْ اَنْ تُؤَدُّوا الْاَمٰنٰتِ اِلٰى اَهْلِهَا ﴾}$$

Lo! Allah commandeth you that ye restore deposits to their owners. Prophet called Uthman and returned him the key. He recited this verse and said O tribe of Talha this key will remain forever among you. Any

---

[1] Sahih Bukhari

offender can take that. This key is not given by me but Allah gave it to you.

Jubair bin Mutam says that Gabriel (blessings of Allah be upon him) came to Prophet and requested him so long this house remains this service should be done by family of Sheeba. None should ever share this honor with them. None should terminate them from this service unless they agree. None should try to change their custom on which Prophet as well as righteous caliphs acted upon. As the verdicts have been given by the Scholars of Makkah.Sheikh Salih Kamal Hanafi gave verdict that holding the key of Ka'aba, opening and closing and serving is the responsibility of the Family of Sheeba. Prophet called Uthman and handed over the key to him. He said that Allah has given you this key and not me. Then he recited this verse from the holy Quran. 'Lo! Allah commandeth you that ye restore deposits to their owners.'

A good number of interpreters stated that this reached to the state of repeating again and again that this verse was revealed about the Uthman bin Abi Talha on the conquest of Makkah. Prophet told him that this service would continue in your family till the Day of Judgment. Gabriel (blessings of Allah be upon him) said so long this house remains on the surface this service would be their responsibility. The traces of the function of the time of the ignorance are discharged except the custodianship of the Ka'aba. All these traditions show that it is not permissible for those who belive in Allah and the Prophet that he should go against the will of Allah. Prophet and the righteous caliphs have continued the practice of the Prophet. Hence it is not allowed for anybody to terminate the key

Ibn Zahira and other scholars of Makkah are of the opinion that this should not be understood in analogy with other things, since it is the commandment of Allah and his beloved Prophet.[1]

---

[1] *All the above mentioned traditions indicate the honor of the family of Sheeba. May Allah give us inspirations to act accordingly. Rauf Siddiqui.*

The decision of Scholars and Authorities about Ka'aba

It is permissible for the family of Sheeba to get the gifts and cover of Ka'aba as the traditions recorded by Bukhari, ibne Majah, Dar Qutni from Wael. Aisha (May Allah be pleased with her) reported from Prophet that it is allowed that they can stop anybody entering Ka'aba. According to another tradition, Aisha said (May Allah be pleased with her) says that every wife of Prophet entered the Ka'aba except me. Prophet asked her to seek permission from Sheeba. You can be permitted because you have close family terms with them. She contacted them. They came to Prophet saying that the door of Ka'aba cannot be opened at night neither in the days of ignorance nor in the days of Islam. If you say we can open that. Prophet took Aisha (May Allah be pleased with her) holding her hand and asked her to offer her prayers in Hateem.

All the traditions mentioned earlier show that this service would continue in the family of Sheeeba as Prophet ordered about it. Zuhri says that they can use the already used cover of Ka'aba. They can take the gifts of Ka'aba in a decent manner.

Bisher bin Sari writes in "Al Manasik" that Abu Hanifa entered the Ka'aba and offered the prayer and gave 1000 deenar to the family of Sheeba. He said that they are the legitimate key bearers of the House of Allah. Zujaj narrates that Once a man asked Sheeba is it lawful for you to take the gifts of Ka'aba. Sheeba replied him that Prophet did not forbid them.

Sheeba bin Uthman

Fakehi records that Abdur Rehman Zujaj asked Sheeba about the use of the gifts. He replied that it is allowed. Fakehi records in Kitab-e-Makkah that a man came to Umar to ask about the gifts in the Ka'aba for the family of Sheeba. He replied him that it is allowed because holy Prophet did not forbid. In "Tafseer Saalibi" it is written that this verse "Lo! Allah commandeth you that ye restore deposits to their owners" was revealed about Uthman on the Conquest of Makkah. A tradition says that he became Muslim when Prophet gave him the key. This tradition is denied. It is known that he had accepted Islam. He migrated along Amr bin Aas and Khalid bin Walid to Madinah. This is most authentic in this regard. He remained in Madinah till he breathed his last in 662 A.D. (42 Hijrah)

Qistalani records that his name is Uthman bin Talha bin Abdul Uza. He is also called Hajabi he was known as Sheebi since people knew him with reference to Uthman bin Talha. He was the uncle of Uthman. He narrated one tradition from Prophet. His mother's name was Sulafa. Sheeba bin Uthman bin Abdullah had accepted Islam on the day of conquest of Makkah. His company with Prophet is authentic. He narrated one tradition from Prophet. He did not have any child. Many Ashab Seyar and Huffaz Al Hadith wrote his biography.

Ibne Abdul Bir says that Sheeba Uthamn had the Kuniat Abu Uthman. It is said that he had the Kuniat Abu Safia. His father is known as Aoqas who was killed by Ali (May Allah be pleased with him) in the battle of Uhad. Sheeba accepted Islam on the day of the conquest of Makkah. He also participated in the battle of Hunain. It is also said that he accepted Islam on the day of Hunain.

Zubair says that Sheeba came out with Prophet on the day of Hunain that he was non Muslim. He wanted to deceive Prophet on that day. When Prophet was unconscious he came closer to him. Prophet saw him. Allah changed his heart. Prophet put his hand on his bosom and said Do away from Satan. He became Muslim. He fought for Muslims. He is among those who were with Prophet. He became very good Muslim. Prophet gave either him or his nephew sheeeba bin Uthman the key of Ka'aba. He asked him to keep it with him; it will remain till the Day of Judgment unless any transgressor takes it.

Abu Umar says that Sheeba is the grand father of Banu sheeba who was the custodian of Ka'aba. He breathed his last in the final phase of Muaawiya's government in 678 A.D. (59 Hijrah). A few held that he passed away in the times of Yazid. Others have mentioned his name his among Mualifatul Quloob.

Hafiz Ibne Hajr said that he is Sheeba bin Uthman. Ibne Sikn says that the name of his mother was Ummi Jamil. She was the sister of Musab bin Umair.

A number of Muhadithin including Bukhari say that his company with Prophet is authentic. He accepted Islam on the day of the Conquest of Makkah. His father was killed in the battle of Uhad. His daughter was Safia binte Sheeba. Sheeba was among those companions who remained close to the Prophet on the day of Hunain. He wanted to deceive Prophet. When Prophet was unconscious he came closer to him. Prophet saw him. Allah changed his heart and Prophet put his hand on his bosom and said Do away from Satan. He became Muslim. He fought for Muslims. Prophet gave the key of Ka'aba to Uthman bin Talha bin Abi Talha on the day of the Conquest of Makkah. This key was given by the will of Allah to his nephew Sheeba bin Uthman because he was elder. When Uthman migrated, he made his nephew his attorney. When he came back to Makkah he held the key till his death.

Then it remained in his nephew's custody for almost 17 years. In 657A.D. (56 Hijrah) he was succeeded by Musab and his offspring. It had been inherited even in the days of Ignorance. Qusai distributed six things among his sons. Abdu Dar was given the Key. His offspring continued to provide their services till the Conquest of Makkah.

Muhammad bin Sharfuddin Zubairi in his verdicts and Bukhari in his history remarked that eldest member of the family of Sheeba should be given this responsibility. According to the Prophet. he gave the key to Uthman because he was the eldest. When he went to Madinah he gave the key to Ibne Sheeba. When he came back, he held the key till he breathed his last. He was succeeded by his nephew till his death.

The Decision of Authorities and Scholars

Scholars have clarified this issue that the key should be given to the eldest man. Fakehi says that in the presence of elder this should not be given to the younger even if people disagree on the elder one. Similarly he can not be terminated even he is given life imprisonment. It will not be understood on the principle of analogy on other issues. Since Prophet said this thing in this manner. This has been repeated again and again.

Shiekh Muhammad Khattab says that the family of Sheeba will hold the key till the Day of Judgment. Only a disbeliever will deny that. Prophet clearly said that this will remain forever in their family,only an offender can take it from them. It was supported by Gabriel (blessings of Allah peace be upon him) that key shall be held by this family till the Day of Judgment.

It was also practiced by the righteous caliphs. Abdullah bin Sheeba went to Sulaman bin Abdul Malik to complain against Khalid bin Abdullah the mayor of the city of Makkah. He said that Khalid harrased me. He treated him gentelly and kept him with honor. He wrote a letter to mayor to forbid him to hurt him. Abdullah bin Sheeba gave him the letter. He did not read the letter and beated him again with Soljan. He again went to Sulaman and informed him. He called him on in the mosque. He gathered the people and announced that the Mayor would be beaten. His hands were chopped down and brought him to Syria in fetters.

Another minister requested a concession in the punishment. He reviewed and made concession in that. He should be given 2000 dinars. He came Makkah along with the Qazi. He brought the Mayor to the mosque and beated him. He was paid 2000 dinar. A meeting was held to appreciate the act of the king and wrote a letter of thanks. They said that the Mayor deserved that because he ignored the saying of our Holy Prophet. Who said respect the mosque of Al Haram and the key bearer. All the poets condemned the act of the Mayor. The family of Sheeba reports an event that Abu Hanifa visited the Ka'aba. He came out and said that they are the descendents of Sheeba. They will hold the key till the Day of Judgment. It has also been recorded by Bishr bin Sari, Fakehi and Majdrose Abadi. Abu Hanifa said that they are the key bearers and none would share them. Imam Malik says that this was given to them by Prophet. None would share them. Abu Hanifa was born in 699 A.D. (80 Hijrah) and died in 767 A.D. (150 Hijrah). Imam Malik was born in 709 (90 Hijrah) and died in 795 A.D. (179 hijrah). They were in the era of Hisham bin Abdul Malik.

The description by both the Imams show that the Banu Sheeba were present in their eras. Many Interpreters of Qur'an have mentioned it.

Lo! Allah commandeth you that ye restore deposits to their owners. Was this revealed about the family of Sheeba? Azraqi says he lived till 854 (240 Hijrah) Zubair bin Bukar said Banu Talha became the custodian of the Ka'aba. He passed away in 869 A.D. (270 Hijrah) Ibne Hazm Zahri says that he died in 1064 A.D. (456 Hijrah).

The scholars say that this responsibility should continue in the family Sheeba till the Day of Judgment. Hafiz Ibn Abdul Bir says that Sheeba is the grand father of Banu Sheeba. They were given the responsibility to bear the key of Ka'aba. Ibn Abdul Bir passed away in 1070 A.D. (463 Hijrah) Muhib Tabri says that Prophet said "O tribe of Talha you are given responsibility to bear the key of Ka'aba. It will remain forever in your family".

Tabri passed away in 1203 A.D. (600Hijrah) this was recorded by Ibn Aseer. He passed away in 1206 A.D. (603 Hijrah). Baghawy writes in his Tafseer that the family of sheeba would have the key till the day of Judgment. He passed away in 1235 A.D. (633 Hijrah). Qalqatandi reports every thing. He passed away in 1321 A.D. (721 Hijrah) Majd Din Faroz Abadi says that the family of sheeba will bear the key of Ka'aba till the day of Judgment. He passed away in 1414 A.D. (817 Hijrah).

Ibne Hajr Asqalani says the family of Sheeba is the key bearer of Ka'aba. He passed away in 1449 A.D. (852 Hijrah). Khateeb Shrunbini writes in his book 'Al Sirajul Munir' that the family of Sheeba is the key bearer of Ka'aba till the day of Judgment. He passed away in 1366 A.D. (768 Hijrah). Ismaeel Haqqi Boroswi also said the similar thing. He passed away in 1688 A.D. (1100 Hijrah). The Muhashi of tafseer Jalalain says that the family of Sheeba is the bearer of the key of Ka'aba. He lived till the 12th Hijrah. Ameer Malik says in 'Al Majmooe' that none would share them in the services of Ka'aba.

They Key Bearers of Ka'aba

I have collected the names of the key bearers and Shiekh of mosque of Al Haram. It has been the custom from the days of Ignorance that the title of Sheikh is given to the key bearer of Ka'aba. One of them is Sheikh Ahmad bin Wailam bin Muhammad Sheebi. His surname was Muhiuddin and family name was Abul Abbas. He was in the era of Sultan Uthman Khan. He held the key for 40 years. Sheikh Ahmad Sheebi used to call Sultan Uthman Khan an august and glrorious king. When he went to the court of the king he was respected much. Many historians of Ottomam Empire have recorded that he was succeeded by Sheikh Ahmad bin Salih Sheeba in 1356 A.D. (757 Hijrah). His family name was Abul Fadal Sheebi. He is known as leading Muhadith. He passed away in 1359 A.D. (759Hijrah).

Many key bearers went to the King in the era of Al Uthman. Sheikh Salman bin Muhammad Sheebi went to Madinah. From there he went to Syria. He met the sholars there. Then he went to Egypt where he met Muhammad Ali Pasha. He was respected a lot and was given many gifts. When the key was given to his brother Sheikh Abdullah bin Muhammad, he went to Sultan Ghazi Abdul Majid Khan. He treated him well. He was succeeded by his brother Sheikh Ali bin Muhammad bin Zainul Abideen Alsheebi came to the Sultan Ghazi Abdul Majeed Khan and he was respected a lot.

He went to Sheikh Abdul Qadir bin Ali bin Muhamad Sultan Abdul Hamid Khan. He was respected too. Then Sheikh Zain bin Abdullah bin Muhammad came in 926 A.D. (313 Hijrah) he was given much respect by the King. The author of the book went to see the capital of Ottoman empire many times. I visited in 1833 A.D (1249 H), 1879 A.D (1296 H), 1908 A.D (1326H), 1913 A.D (1332H). I was respected and honored much. Many medals were given to me. I was given the first Medal in 1897 A.D (1315 H). then I was given in 1898 A.D (1316 H) Nishan-e-Majeedi. The third one was given in 1901 A.D (1319 H) the fourth one was given in 1914 (1333 H). I was also given Bashir Khurshid by the govt. of Iran in 1899 A.D (1317H). All sultans from Aal-e-Uthman always respected them. The scholars of Makkah are before us. We thank Allah many times for this honor. The geneology of Banu Sheeba meets the geneology of our Holy Prophet at Qusai. Historians and genealogists agree that the geneology of Qusai meets Adnan. And his lineage meets to Ismaeel and Ibrahim (blessings of Allah be upon them). Therefore the family of Sheeba is the descendents of Ibrahim (blessings of Allah be upon him). The family of sheeba is proud of the honor that they meet in the lineage at Qusai with the Holy Prophet. I am thankful to Allah Almighty on the completion of this book. All the blessings on the Prophet Muhammad (peace and blessings of Allah be upon him) and his companions. The author of the book ended the book on the amalgamation of the lineage with the Holy Prophet. I am also honored with the description of the lineage of the Holy Prophet so that it becomes a source of bountiful blessings for me.

Lineage of Holy Prophet Muhammad
(peace and blessings of Allah be upon him)

Muhammad bin Abdullah bin Abdul Mutalib bin Hashim bin Qusai bin
Kilab bin Mura bin Kaab bin Looi bin Ghalib bin Fahr bin Malik bin
Nadr bin Kinanah bin Khuzaima bin Madrakah bin Ilyas bin Midr bin
Nazar bin Maad bin Adnan. The remaining details are given in the
lineage of the family of Sheeba. By the blessings of Allah, the translation
has been accomplished besides my engagements in the ministry. May
Allah bless me, my family, my city, my country with this work? Save
us from the ill intentions of our enemies. Aameen!

Rauf Siddiqui.

Viewing of Ka'aba is a Worship

The readers should be happy to see the following pictures of Ka'aba
which have never been published before. Here are some invalueable
pictures showing the inside of Ka'aba, the keys of Ka'aba and the
family of Sheeba. I am thankful to the family of Sheeba particularly
Abdur Rehman Salih Zainul Abideen Sheebi who provided me these
pictures. In addition to that I am also grateful to Ibrahim Muhammad
Umar Bux and Mazhar Jamali who helped me in collecting these
pictures.

Rauf Siddiqui.

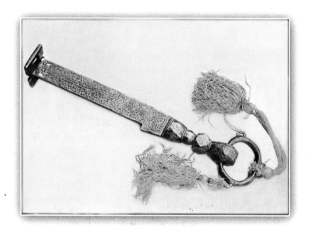

Some of the pictures of the keys of
Holy Ka'aba

The former custodian of The Two Holy Mosques,
King Faisal is seen participating in the repair work of
the Holy Ka'aba. He has exerted a lot of efforts in the
expansion of The Two Holy Mosques

Picture of the well Zamzam from where the water is over flowing

This is the picture of the water of Zamzam which is
flowing in stones

It is the picture of the interior portion of the Holy Ka'aba

History
of Ka'aba

This is the interior part of the Holy Ka'aba.
The people who are blessed by Allah are participating
in the repair work of the Holy Ka'aba

This is the gate of the Ka'aba which is known as the gate
of At-touba (repentance) there is a ladder which links it
to the roof of the Holy Ka'aba

The gate of the Ka'aba is open which gets the light
through the lamp

The marble board which shows where the Holy Prophet
offered prayers after the removal of all idols from Holy Ka'aba
at the time of the Conquest of Makkah

A memorable picture of Sheikh Dr. Saleh Zainul Abideen
bin Abdullah bin Abdul Qadir Shaib while he is praying inside
the Holy Ka'aba

This picture shows the flowing of the flooded water inside the Holy
Ka'aba while the people going around it

This is the picture which shows the important parts
of Holy Ka'aba

الكعبة المشرفة

(قبلة المسلمين)

١ – الحجر الأسود
٢ – باب الكعبة
٣ – الميزاب (مزراب الرحمة)
٤ – الشاذَروان
٥ – حجر إسماعيل (الحطيم)
٦ – المُلتَزَم
٧ – مقام سيدنا إبراهيم
٨ – ركن الحجر الأسود
٩ – الركن اليماني
١٠ – الركن الشامي
١١ – الركن العراقي
١٢ – ستار الكعبة
١٣ – خط المرمر البني

The picture of Holy Ka'aba indicates its different places

The memorable picture of the footprints of the prophet Ibrahim
(Blessings of Allah be upon him) on the place of Ibrahim

The closeup picture of the footprints of the prophet Ibrahim
(Blessings of Allah be upon him) which are
more visible and clear

This picture shows the Black Stone

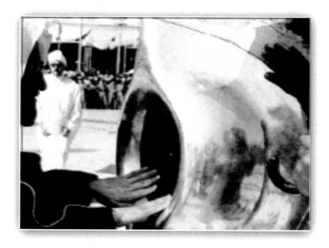

The man touches the Black Stone

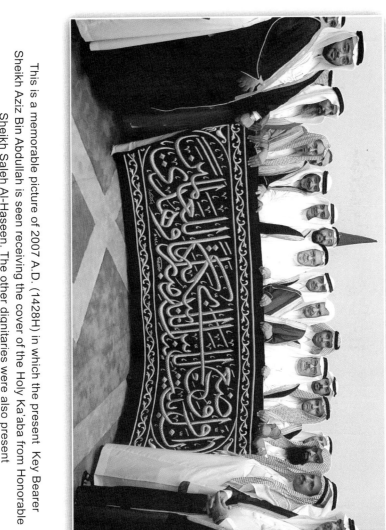

This is a memorable picture of 2007 A.D. (1428H) in which the present Key Bearer Sheikh Aziz Bin Abdullah is seen receiving the cover of the Holy Ka'aba from Honorable Sheikh Saleh Al-Haseen. The other dignitaries were also present

سماحة الشيخ عاصم بن عبد الله الشيبي رحمه الله اثناء تسلمه كسوة الكعبة المشرفة

The former key bearer, Honorable Sheikh Asim bin Abdullah Al Shaibi is seen receiving the cover of Ka'aba along with other elites.

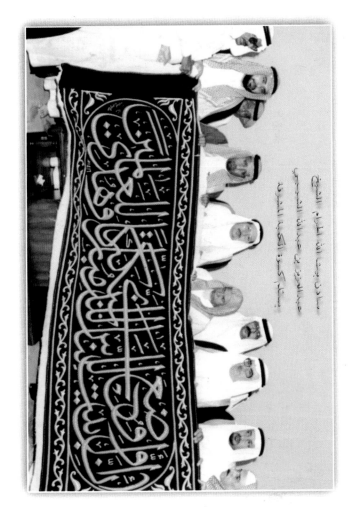

In this memorable picture the present Key Bearer of Ka'aba, Sheikh Abdul Aziz bin Abdullah is seen receiving the cover of the Holy Ka'aba

The former Key Bearer of Ka'aba, Sheikh Taha bin Abdullah Al
Sahibi (May Allah grant him His Mercy) is seen receiving the
cover of the Holy Ka'aba

Sheikh Muhammad Amin bin Abdullah Al Shaib (May Allah grant him His Mercy) is seen receiving the cover of the Holy Ka'aba

History of Ka'aba

Sheikh Muhammad Taha bin Abdullah Al Shaibi, Sheikh Muhammad bin Muhammad Saleh and Sheikh Muhammad Amin Bin Abdullah Al Shaibi (May Allah grant them mercy) are seen coming out of the House of Allah along with their servants

146

The former key bearer of the Holy Ka'aba Sheikh Taha bin Abdullah
Al Shaibi (May Allah grant him His Mercy) was born in 1914 A.D.
(1333H) and passed away in 1986 A.D. (1407H)

History
of Ka'aba

The former key brear of Ka'aba Sheikh Abdullah Qadir bin Mohammad
Ali Al Shaibi appears with some of his grand sons and a group of
Egyptian doctors and politicians at Cairo in the year.
1932 A.D. (1353H)

The former key bearer of the Ka'aba and author of the book
"The History of Ka'aba" Sheikh Mohammad Saleh bin Ahmad Zainul
Abideen Al Shaibi. He was born in 1854 A.D. (1271 H)
and died in 1916 A.D. (1335 H)

The former key bearaer of the House of Allah Sheikh Muhammad
bin Muhammad Al Shaibi is seen standing in front of the
gate of the House of Allah

This is the picture of the former key bearer of Ka'aba Sheikh Abdullah bin Abdul Qadir bin Al Shaibi, who was born in 1879 A.D (1296H) and died in 1952 A.D. (1371H). He held different positions in the government of Late King Abdul Aziz. He was also the member of the state council.

The former key bearer of Ka'aba Al Sheikh Abdul Qadir bin Muhammad Ali Al Shaibi (May Allah grant him His Mercy) was born 1804 A.D. (1271 H) and died in 1930 A.D. (1351H)

In this memorial picture you can see the members of the ruling King family as well as the family of Al Shaib who are incharge of Ka'aba in the delegation of Al Hajaz who came to confirm allegiance to the crown prince Saud bin Abdul Aziz at the palace in the city of Riayadh at the time of king Abdul Aziz(starting from right) Sheikh Abdul Wahab the deputy key bearer of Kaaba as well as Sheikh Abdullah Al Sahibi and behind him his son Sheikh Taha Al Sahibi

Picture of the Key bearer of Ka'aba Sheikh Dr. Saleh Zain Al Abideen bin Abdullah bin Abdul Qadir Al Shaibi along with his son Abdul Rahman bin Saleh Al Shaibi

The former key bearer of Ka'aba
Sheikh Abdul Qadir bin Taha Al Shaibi

The picture of the former key bearer of Ka'aba Al Shiekh Asim bin
Abdul Al Shaibi (May Allah grant him His Mercy). He was born in
1921 A.D. (1340H) and died in 1992 A.D. (1413H)

The picture of former key bearer Al Sheikh Talha bin Hassan
Al Shaibi (May Allah grant him mercy). He was born in
1921 A.D. (1340 H) He died in 2005 A.D. (1426 H)

This picture shows Al Sheikh Abdul Rehamn Al Shaibi standing along with minister of the industry and commerce of Sindh, Rauf Siddiqui.

This picture shows the present key bearer Al Sheikh Abdul Aziz bin Abdullah Qadir Al Shaibi sitting along with the chief justice of Pakistan Abdul Hamid Dogar and with minister of Industry and commerce of Sindh, Rauf Siddiqui

This picture shows the present key bearer Al Sheikh Abdul Aziz bin
Abdul Qadir Al Shaibi sitting along with minister of the industry
and commerce of Sindh Rauf Siddiqui on 16th August, 2008

This picture shows Rauf Siddiqui standing with
Yaqoob Memon and Mazhar Jamali

This picture shows the present key bearer of Ka'aba
Al Sheikh Abdul Aziz bin Abdullah bin Abdul Qadir Al Shaibi
carrying the key of the Holy Ka'aba

This picture shows the present key bearer of Ka'aba Al Sheikh Abdul
Aziz bin Abdullah bin Abdul Qadir Al Shaibi is seen
opening the door of Holy Ka'aba

This picture shows Rauf Siddiqui holding the hand of the present
key bearer of the Holy Ka'aba Al Sheikh Abdul Aziz bin Abdullah
bin Abdul Qadir Al Shaibi at his residence in 2005 A.D.

A soul inspiring beautiful view of the Holy Ka'aba during prayer

An Amazing view of the mosque Al Haram during prayer

The imaginary view of reconstruction and expansion phases of Ka'aba during different epoches

The firstever published, historic and memorable
picture of walls of Holy Ka'aba without covers.

History
of Ka'aba

Letter from President of the Council of Ministers Lebanese Republic

LEBANESE REPUBLIC
President of the Council of Ministers

H.E. Mr. Rauf Siddiqui
Minister of Industries and Commerce
Government of Sindh

Beirut, March 12, 2009

Excellency,

I received with much interest your book History of Ka aba. I thank you for all the efforts you are making to spread the word of God by doing deep researches in order to clarify aspects relating to the History of Ka aba. I support your endeavours and wish you further success in the future.

Please accept the assurances of my high consideration.

Fuad Siniora

Letter from Prime Minister of People's Democratic Republic of Algeria

الجُمهُورِيَة الجَزائرِيَة الدّيمُقراطية الشّعُبية

الوزير الأول

إلـــى

21 جويلية 2009

السـيد رؤوف صـديقـي،
وزير الصناعة والتجارة بحُكومة
مقاطعة السند بجمهورية باكستان الإسلامية،

معالي الوزير،

يشرفني إشعاركم باستلامي لمؤلفكم القيم الذي أبتم، رغـم
مسؤولياتكم ومهامكم الوزارية، إلا أن تخصصوه "لتاريخ الكعبة الشريفة"
وتكرموا بإهدائي نسخة منه، وقد سعدت كثيرا بهذه الإلتفاتة الطيبة.

وإذ أهنئكم على هذا الإنجاز الكبير وعلى ما بذلتموه من جهد في
التأريخ لهذا المعلم الإسلامي العظيم، الذي سيكون إن شاء الله، مرجعا نادرا
للتعريف بجوانب هامة تتصل ببيت الله، فإنه لا يسعني إلا أن أشكركم
جزيل الشكر على كرم عنايتكم، متمنيا لكم موفور الصحة والسعادة،
وكل التوفيق في مهامكم النبيلة.

Thank you for your kind
attention and with my
best regards

Translation of Letter from Prime Minister of People's Democratic Republic of Algeria

EMBASSY OF THE
PEOPLE'S DEMOCRATIC REPUBLIC OF ALGERIA
ISLAMABAD

سـفارة الجمهـورية
الجـزائـريـة الـديـموقـراطيـة الشعبـيـة
اسـلام آبـاد

(COURTESY TRANSLATION)

People's Democratic Republic of Algeria

The Prime Minister   *Algiers, 21ˢᵗ February 2009.*

His Excellency
Mr. Raouf Siddiqui
Sindh Minister for Industry and Commerce
Government of the Islamic Republic of Pakistan

Excellency,

I have the honor to acknowledge with great pleasure receipt of a copy of your excellent work on the history of the sacred MEKKAHA EL CHARI FA which you have so kindly sent to me and also for your kind dedication that you devoted to it despite your daily Ministerial hectic schedule.

While wishing you for the accomplishment of the work and the efforts that you have deployed to this historic Islamic monument which, I am sure, will be Inshaalah a significant reference for the popularization of this sacred Qaaba. I can only be thankful to you and wish you good health, happiness and full success in your noble functions.

Please accept, Excellency, the assurances of my highest consideration.

Ahmed Ouyahia

History
of Ka'aba

**Letter from The Head of the
Cabinet of the President of
the French Republic**

*Le Chef de Cabinet
du Président de la République*

Monsieur Rauf SIDDIQUI
Minister
Industries & Commerce
Government of Sindh

Paris, le **2 5 FEV. 2009**

Monsieur le Ministre,

Le Président de la République française a bien reçu le courrier par lequel vous avez eu la très aimable pensée de lui dédicacer le livre, intitulé "History of Ka'aba", du Cheik Muhammad Sahleh Zainul AAbedin Al-Shebi, dont vous avez assuré la publication.

Monsieur Nicolas SARKOZY m'a chargé de vous remercier vivement de votre envoi, auquel il a particulièrement été sensible.

Je puis vous assurer de l'intérêt et de l'attention avec lesquels il a été pris connaissance du remarquable travail de recherche historique consacré à ce haut lieu sacré de l'Islam.

Je vous prie d'agréer, Monsieur le Ministre, l'expression de ma haute considération.

Cédric GOUBET

Référence à rappeler
SCP/CdO/C025619

168

Translation of Letter from The Head of the Cabinet of the President of the French Republic

The Head of the Cabinet of the
President of the Republic

Paris, February 25, 2009

Reference : SCP/Cdo/C025619

Dear Minister,

The President of the French republic has duly received your letter in which you have very kindly thought to dedicate him the book entitled "History of Ka'aba" by Sheikh Muhammad Sahled Zainul Aabedin, whose publication you have ensured.

Mr. Nicolas Sarkozy has directed me to thank you warmly for you parcel, for which he was particularly touched.

Let me assure you of the interest and the attention given to this remarkable work of historic research devoted to this highly sacred place of Islam.

Please accept, dear Minister, the assurances of my highest consideration.

Cédric GOUBET

Mr. Rauf Siddiqui
Minister for Industries and Commerce
Government of Sindh

Letter from the President The Republic of Tunisia

قرطاج في 2 مارس 2009

الجمـهـوريـة التونـسـيـة
الرَّثـٰيـسْ

السيد رؤوف صديق

تلقيت بامتنان كتابكم القيّم بعنوان "تاريخ بيت الله".

وإذ أتوجّه إليكم بجزيل الشكر وبالغ الثناء على جميل العناية ولطف الإهداء، فإني أقدّر جهودكم المحمودة في تأليف هذا الكتاب بعدّة لغات وما تضمنه من معلومات ضافية حول تاريخ الكعبة الشّريفة وإبراز خصائصها المميّزة، مكبرين تنويهكم بمخطوط الكاتب التونسي محمد صالح زين العابدين الشابي حول تاريخ الكعبة المقدّسة.

مع تَشجيعي وأطيب تمنياتي لكم بآطراد التوفيق والنجاح.

زين العابدين بن علي

السيد رؤوف صديق
وزير الصناعة والتجارة بحكومة السّند

Translation of Letter from The President The Republic of Tunisia

Unofficial translation

The Republic of Tunisia
The President

Carthage, Mars 2nd, 2009

Mr Rauf Siddik,

With gratitude, I received your valuable book entitled "The History of Kaaba".

Addressing to you my best thanks and huge praise for the beautiful care and the kind presenting, I would express my consideration for your commendable efforts afford editing this book in several languages, including plentiful informations around the history of Kaaba Charif and showing its distinguished characteristics. Then, I would hail your reference to the manuscript of Tunisian author Mohamed Salah Zine El Abidine Chebbi about the History of Kaaba Charif.

With my encouragements and wishes for steady success.

Zine El Abidine BEN ALI

Mr Rauf Siddik
Minister of Industry and Commerce
of Government of Sindh

Letter from the President of
United States of America

THE WHITE HOUSE
WASHINGTON

July 31, 2009

The Honorable M.A. Rauf Siddiqui
Minister of Industries and Commerce
Sindh
PAKISTAN

Dear Mr. Minister:

I would like to extend my deepest thanks and appreciation for your kind gift.

As our two nations work to address the new and complex challenges facing our world, I am hopeful about what our countries can accomplish together.

Again, thank you for the wonderful gift.

Sincerely,